Collaborative Research in Second Language Education

Edited by Mike Beaumont and Teresa O'Brien

Trentham Books

Stoke on Trent, UK and Sterling, USA

Trentham Books Limited

Westview House	22883 Quicksilver Drive
734 London Road	Sterling
Oakhill	VA 20166-2012
Stoke on Trent	USA
Staffordshire	
England ST4 5NP	

First published 2000

British Library Cataloguing-in-Publication Data
A catalogue record for this book is available from the
British Library

1 85856 171 X (paperback)

Designed and typeset by Trentham Print Design Ltd., Chester and printed in
Great Britain by Biddles Limited, Guildford.

Collaborative Research in Second Language Education

*In memory of our parents, William and Ethel O'Brien,
and Mary Beaumont.*

Contents

Introduction

This book has four major themes. Firstly, and perhaps most importantly, it is about **research** – research that is intended to have a significant impact on classroom practice, and therefore be of direct benefit to teachers and learners. This impact may be direct, in that the research has been carried out by teachers themselves in their own classrooms. It may be less direct, in that the research is concerned with teacher education, distance learning or test development. However, throughout the book, voices are heard from all the levels of the educational 'stack', as Woodward (1991) puts it: from pupils and their teachers; from support teachers and their management team; from teacher trainees and their trainers; from students on postgraduate teacher education courses, and their tutors; from research students and their supervisors. We hope this book provides evidence that all those with a direct involvement in the educational process can contribute positively to classroom research.

The early planning for the book took place at a time when the value of educational research had become a matter of public debate in the UK. In a lecture given to the Teacher Training Agency (TTA) in 1996, Hargreaves argued that educational research, as practised and produced by educational researchers had failed to provide a sound evidence-base for teaching, and recommended that teachers play a more central role in setting the agenda for research and carrying it out. Currently, the TTA, partly under the influence of Hargreaves, is funding collaborative work involving local authorities, teachers and teacher educators. The TTA web page (http://www.teach-tta.gov.uk/research/evidence/rebp.htm) points out that teachers who effectively use research and evidence to improve their practice and raise attainment 'should be seen as equal partners with academic researchers in the process of producing evidence about teaching and using it to raise standards'.

This brings us to our second theme: **collaboration**. The book describes a wide variety of projects arising out of the work of a single group of colleagues – the members of the Centre for English Language Studies in Education (CELSE) in the School of Education at the University of Manchester. It is therefore about colleagues working together. More importantly, though, it is about those teacher educators working with others in different sectors of education. The notion of the ìcritical friendî is central. As teacher educators in a university, we see ourselves as practical classroom teachers and as researchers. The work reported here shows us interacting with teacher-researchers in various supporting, guiding and learning roles. Moreover, the writing itself has been collaborative, allowing us to reflect on our joint experience, understand it better, and relate it to current educational theory.

Each chapter is co-written by members of CELSE and colleagues from schools, educational authorities, teacher training colleges and other universities. We hope to show how learning occurs through practice-based research and how the collaboration of teacher-researchers and academic teacher educators can lead to better informed classroom practice and to the development of educational theory. We believe with Ainscow (1997) that the literature of educational research can provide an important stimulus for reflection on practice and therefore for professional development, but that such research should be treated by practitioners not as a prescription for practice but as a contribution to the resources upon which we can all draw in order to refine our knowledge and understanding of teaching. A third theme, therefore, is **professional development**. Learning how to teach is a career-long activity. Successful teachers reflect on and examine their classroom practice constantly. The same is, or should be, true of teacher educators. The collaborative projects reported here are not simply about doing research. They are about the professional development that accrues, for all involved, when colleagues work together to do that research.

Fourthly, the book is about **language education**. The language in this case is English, but the language education is of two kinds. A number of the papers in this volume are focused on second language education, that is on contexts where the language being learnt is the medium of education. Other papers describe projects in contexts where English is being taught as a foreign language – that is, where English is not the medium of communication. The book is therefore international in its scope, reporting on work in seven countries on three continents. We hope, as a consequence, to make connections between two dimensions of the language education field which traditionally have been seen as quite separate, even incompatible. Further, we would like to place this work within a cross-curricular perspective, as we feel that language education is too often perceived as the province of language specialists, instead of being seen as an essential element of all education.

The book falls into four parts. It begins in **Part 1** with an account of an in-service programme in which university tutors helped to give more than forty language support teachers their first experience of action research. Chapter 1 outlines the context, design and evaluation of the programme; chapters 2 to 4 then report on three individual projects within it, set in reception, primary and secondary classrooms. **Part 2** describes three more practitioner-based research projects. The context for Chapter 5 is also language support but on this occasion the project developed from an electronic link between university students on a Masters programme and bilingual pupils in a nearby secondary school. Chapters 6,7 and 8 introduce the international dimension, giving accounts of projects in Namibia, Korea and Bulgaria. Collaboration between the Namibian Ministry of Education and the Universities of Manchester and East Anglia led to the creation of distance training materials for primary teachers on an upgrading programme. The authors explore the ways in which a practice-based inquiry cycle operated at various levels during the development of the project. Chapter 7 describes how an educational researcher used quantitative methods to compare teacher and pupil perceptions of the teaching of writing skills in Korean secondary schools and then supported a small group of teachers in their attempts to introduce innovative practices in their own classrooms. In Chapter 8, we visit Bulgaria where action research projects have been used to develop and chart the progress of cultural awareness materials in the foreign language classroom.

Part 3 includes accounts of projects which have used other research methods to examine teacher development programmes, two of which involve distance education. Chapter 9 takes us to Greece where distance materials designed originally for international use on CELSEís Masters programme are now being used by Greek teachers of English whose course is tutored by the Hellenic Open University. The writers are concerned to capture the emerging educational culture which has been created through the collaboration of two universities. Chapter 10 deals with a project in which Russian teachers were supported in writing localised distance learning materials. Using a framework for understanding personal change, it too examines the meeting of two educational cultures. Chapter 11 reports on collaborative work between Manchester University and a cluster of Polish teacher training colleges in the Łódź region, in which the production of video training materials grew into collaboration over doctoral research. Concluding this section, Chapter 12 returns to the UK context and investigates the reactions of mainstream subject teachers to an in-service programme on supporting the language development of bilingual pupils.

In **Part 4** we look at the world of testing. Chapter 13 reports on an ongoing research project into English paired oral examinations which is concerned to explore the communication norms which underlie assessorsí judgements. Chapter 14 examines the effects of a six year in-service programme in the design, administration and marking of achievement and proficiency tests in teacher training colleges in Poland, drawing parallels between the process of test development and that of undertaking classroom research. Finally, in Chapter 15, an innovation in testing based on research into genres, currently being trialled in Hungary, is described and analysed.

A feature of many of the studies reported here is that the research was carried out without any special funding by teachers working under very pressured conditions in often quite difficult circumstances, and by university staff working in the equally pressured conditions of a self-funded unit which derives its principal income from teaching but operates within a research-oriented culture. We hope that the book will encourage others to take a similar learning path although their circumstances, too, may be difficult.

References

Ainscow, M. (1997) Would it work in theory? Arguments for practitioner research in the special needs field. In C. Clark et al *Theorising Special Education*. London: Routledge.

Hargreaves, D. (1996) Teaching as a research-based profession. *Teacher Training Agency Annual Lecture*.

Woodward, T. (1991) *Models and Metaphors in Language Teacher Training*. Cambridge: Cambridge University Press.

PART 1: One project: three studies

CHAPTER ONE

Seeing if it makes a difference:
a team-based approach to practitioner research with language support teachers

Mike Beaumont
University of Manchester

Mary Coates and Ian Jones
Language for Educational Access Project, Rochdale

Introduction

This chapter, which gives the background context for chapters 2-4, tells the story of a group of teachers and teacher educators who were already working together fruitfully. It is about how the idea of practitioner-based research emerged from that co-operation, and how the principle of collaboration operated throughout a project that gave a large team of teachers their first formal experience of doing action research, and a small team of teacher educators their first experience of facilitating a project on such a scale. This story does not claim to say anything new about practice-based research, nor does it claim that the project was 'successful' in any objective sense. We feel it is important because, firstly, the work that language support teachers do deserves a wider audience; secondly, support teachers are, by virtue of the collaborative nature of their work, almost uniquely placed to stimulate dialogue about, and partnership in, teaching; and thirdly, we want to present a positive example of the ways in which classroom teachers, teachers in management roles, and tutors in higher education can work together for their mutual benefit. That partnership is represented in a tangible way by the joint authorship of this chapter. Mary Coates and Ian Jones work for the Language for Educational Access Project (LEAP) and Mike Beaumont teaches at the University of Manchester.

I

A Bit of History

Because five other chapters in this book relate to language support work in British schools, we feel it would be useful to give a brief history of its development. The provision of language support has been a significant feature of the British state education system since the 1960s. Changes in the terms used to refer to pupils in British schools whose first language is not English have reflected how the demographic, educational and political ground has shifted in the intervening period. Early references were to 'the teaching of English to' *immigrants*, in recognition of the influx of families from, principally, the Caribbean and the Asian sub-continent in answer to Britain's post-war employment needs. By the late 1970s, educationalists had begun to refer to children of *ethnic minority* origin, as it became important to recognise that the majority of children from such groups were second generation, that is, born in the UK. Reference to *multi-cultural education* also became common, sensitive teachers realising that, although the teaching of English was an important priority, the permanent presence of new cultures in Britain had wider curricular implications, affecting the education of all children. The use of the term *ESL (English as a Second Language) pupils* was gradually superseded during the 1980s by the more positive *bilingual learners*, in acknowledgement of the importance of pupils' existing language repertoires and also of the need for schools to encourage their continuing development. While reference to bilingual learners remains in current use, talk of teaching *English as an Additional Language* (EAL) has become prevalent recently, since the linguistic background of many children means that, as the language of schooling, English is being acquired as at least a third language. It also reflects the notion of *additive* rather than *subtractive* bilingualism. As a result, there are now moves to define more precisely the parameters of EAL, as opposed to straightforwardly bilingual contexts, and thereby establish EAL as a distinct and separate field of study. For a succinct survey of current developments, see Leung (1996).

Changes can also be charted in the perceived roles and in the nature of the work of language support teachers over the same period. Three major trends can be observed. In the early years, many Local Education Authorities (LEAs) set up specialist *language centres*, to which newly arrived immigrant children were sent until they were considered linguistically competent enough in English to attend 'normal' classes. This model had a number of obvious disadvantages, not the least of which was the isolation of the children and their teachers from the mainstream curriculum and from interaction with native English speaking pupils. A number of authorities eschewed this model from the start, recognising the need for bilingual pupils to be as fully integrated into school life as possible. In these cases, language support units were set up within individual schools, children being 'withdrawn' for language teaching for periods of time appropriate to their perceived level of linguistic need. However, this approach could also result in the disjunction of language support work from mainstream educational concerns, particularly where it was provided by peripatetic teachers, who could only spend a proportion of their working week in a particular school.

The third and by now the most widely accepted model is for support to be provided within the context of mainstream classes (Bourne, 1989). Potentially, all parties benefit. The learners have full time access to the curriculum, to native speaker models, and to appropriate language support. The support teacher can diagnose and act very specifically on the needs of particular learners in particular subjects and the subject teacher becomes much more aware of the needs of learners of EAL and of techniques that make the curriculum more accessible to them. In most examples of best practice, support teachers work through an LEA controlled support service, which co-ordinates provision across all the authority's schools, both primary and secondary, thus providing consistency and mitigating possible fragmentation or duplication.

It is within this general context that the Project reported in this paper was carried out. The more specific context was that of the Language for Educational Access Project (LEAP) in Rochdale.[1]

The Research Project

LEAP and the Centre for English Language Studies in Education (CELSE) at the University of Manchester have been working together since 1989, when teachers from the LEAP service were invited to provide input on language support for initial trainees on a Postgraduate Certificate in Education (PGCE) course. A more substantial phase of co-operation began in 1992, when the LEAP service engaged CELSE staff to run a number of in-service courses for all their support tutors. On completion of this phase in June 1996, the LEAP management decided to request a further module on Classroom Research, based on the need to investigate the impact of staff development programmes, including the input from CELSE, and to evaluate how support staff had begun to translate new knowledge and techniques into practice. The decision was also based on the view that EAL teachers are already researchers in the following ways:

- EAL teachers work with other teachers in partnership and have opportunities to evaluate, analyse and triangulate in an atmosphere of trust and professionalism which has been built up over time

- EAL teachers' work involves developing strategies and techniques, the outcomes of which need to be evaluated for the benefit of pupils' language and learning development

- EAL teachers are involved in the process of influencing change in the practice of mainstream teachers which also requires a constant need to evaluate

- the research base for EAL in the mainstream UK context is weak, having relied heavily on general ELT theory – this lack of an appropriate research and pedagogical base has meant that a considerable amount of in-class development has been necessary

- EAL teachers' work involves proving their effectiveness against targets and value for money in order to justify central government funding.

The Project was designed in three phases. The first, consisting of two half day sessions, was the Planning Phase. In the first session, the concept of action/practitioner-based research was described and discussed. We began with a sample case study taken from Hopkins (1985: 17ff), selected as being particularly appropriate to our context as it involved collaboration between mainstream and learning support teachers. We then considered and discussed definitions of action research from Cohen and Manion (1994) and Elliott (1991), contrasting action research with 'applied research' and stressing in particular that action research should not only be small-scale, context-based, collaborative, participatory, and self-evaluative but that it should also work to improve the rationality, justice, and quality of classroom practice.

The framework finally suggested to the teachers was based on Allwright's *exploratory practice* model, developed with teachers and teacher educators in Brazil. 'The basic process advocated for 'exploratory work' ...is one of using already familiar pedagogic activities to investigate teacher and learner 'puzzles" (Allwright, 1993:131). The model suggests eight procedural stages (seen below in Figure 1). In the initial input session, teachers were given the Allwright stages in jumbled order and asked to sequence them. Feedback on the task led us to an amended model which can be seen in Figure 1.

Allwright (1993)	CELSE (1996-97)
1 Identify a puzzle area	1 Identify a puzzle area
2 Refine your thinking about that puzzle area	2 Formulate a question
3 Select a particular topic to focus upon	3 Brainstorm answers and list subsidiary questions to arrive at a a more focused question
4 Find appropriate classroom procedures to explore it	5 Outline in detail the classroom procedures you would use to explore
5 Adapt them to the particular puzzle you want to explore	the puzzle
6 Use them in class	6 Identify suitable data collection procedures
7 Interpret the outcomes	7 Pilot the procedures with a small
8 Decide on their implications and plan accordingly	group of students
	8 Make any necessary improvements
	9 Implement the full study
	10 Report on and evaluate the study

Figure 1: Adaptation of the Allwright Exploratory Practice Model

Additionally, but unspecified by the Allwright framework, teachers were encouraged to identify the nature of the data to be collected during the exploration of their puzzle area. This would be either data which teachers could collect by themselves, for example lesson plans, post-lesson reflective notes, diaries, audio or video recordings, questionnaires and interviews, or data which they could ask colleagues to collect, for example, through observation schedules.

Primary School

1 Will a highly structured spelling approach improve the spelling ability of bilingual pupils?

2 Does the language predicted by the teacher correlate with the actual language produced by bilingual children in Year 3 science lessons?*

3 How can the teacher's questioning technique elicit and enrich children's vocabulary in a Reception class?

4 Would the idea of using a scrapbook succeed in engaging bilingual Reception children more productively during the early morning period?

5 What effect does teacher input have on bilingual pupils' language?

6 Does extra teacher intervention improve bilingual pupils' problem-solving skills?

7 Do ideational frameworks help bilingual pupils in Key Stages 1 and 2 retrieve information for use in speech and writing?*

8 How can the oral component of baseline assessment be made more accessible to bilingual children?

Secondary School

1 Can active learning strategies be used to teach grammar through poetry?

2 Can more independence in maths be achieved by requiring bilingual pupils to read and discuss problems in pairs?

3 Will pupils with both higher and lower level reading skills benefit from a reading enrichment programme?

4 How can pupils' listening skills be improved during the first 5-10 minutes of a lesson?

5 What effects, if any, does the classroom analysis of discoursal features of fairy tales (narrative discourse) have on pupils' production of fairy tales?*

6 Will a focus on cohesive devices help bilingual pupils to produce better structured texts?

Cross-Phase

1 How can bilingual pupils' competence in tackling non-fiction texts be increased in Years 5, 6 and 7?

* reported in this volume.

Figure 2: The research questions

The second session concentrated on the first five steps of the Allwright framework. By this stage, fifteen research groups had been formed, and one of the three university tutors assigned to each group to act as principal facilitator and advisor. So in the second session each tutor tried to assist their groups in identifying a sufficiently focused research question, in specifying the classroom activities they would engage in to generate the data for their research, and the precise form of that data, and in planning when and how they would pilot their projects.

The second phase, also comprising two sessions, was termed the Implementation Phase. By this time, groups were understandably working at different speeds, but the aim was, by the end of this phase, for all groups to have finalised their projects, to have completed their planning, and to have carried out a pilot. The final research questions of the fifteen groups are listed in Figure 2. There were eight primary level investigations, six secondary, and one cross-phase.

Between Phases 2 and 3, the fifteen research projects were carried out, each group being asked to prepare a preliminary report for the next session. Phase 3, Analysis and Evaluation, also consisted of two sessions. In the first, groups reported back to each other orally on the progress of their projects, and submitted their written reports. Video recordings of four of the projects were shown and discussed, and the university tutors provided further input on data analysis. The university tutors also asked the participating teachers to complete a simple, open-ended questionnaire in order to facilitate an initial evaluation of the overall Project. The final session involved the university tutors feeding back on the questionnaire responses and on the participants' reports, and a final evaluation of the whole Project. We present here what we consider to be the most significant and interesting findings from the questionnaire responses.

The Questionnaire
Understanding
Section 1 asked participants to recall their understanding and view of action research after the initial input session. Their responses fell into two categories: first, what might be termed their 'reactions to the idea', and second, their understanding of 'the actual process' of action research. Reactions ranged from finding the idea 'daunting' to feeling 'excited' by

the proposal and being keen to begin. In general, they had liked the idea of being in control of the research process, seeing it as an opportunity to assess the impact of their practice – to 'see if it actually makes a difference', as one participant put it. Three key characteristics of the action research process were recalled: that it was cyclical, that it should be very focused, and that it should be small scale. Despite this, some observed that it had taken them a long time to identify their puzzle area.

Impact

The second section of the questionnaire invited participants to make an initial assessment of the impact of their project on the various parties involved. In terms of effects on the learners, the four most commonly occurring comments were: the collection of data had enabled the teachers to demonstrate that their practice had aided their learners' language development; it had improved the learners' own understanding of the learning process; it had boosted their confidence in handling the language; and it had helped to make the learning more individualised.

On teachers' own practice, four views were again dominant: carrying out the research had provided them with tools to analyse their practice more deeply; they had become more critical of their own practice; it had provided them with a greater awareness of the individuality of their learners; and the research process had improved their monitoring and observation skills.

With respect to the perceived effects of the Project on the support team as a whole, there were three recurring themes: the focused nature of the research had had a substantial effect on teamwork within the groups, building up relationships and enabling them to operate more effectively as a team in school; the project had provoked discussion with support staff in other research groups; and the research had assisted them in organising work with mainstream teachers and in improving the self-esteem of the team within their school.

A crucial aspect of language support teaching is successfully sensitising mainstream teachers and school management teams to language issues affecting bilingual learners across the curriculum. In general, the support teachers thought that the Research Project had helped to raise the profile of EAL learners and language support teachers within the school. In some cases mainstream teachers had shown increased interest in particular language strategies, to the extent that some had developed a vested interest in the success of a project. A second effect was improved relationships between support and mainstream staff. Not only had the projects required the support and collaboration of mainstream teachers, but they had helped partnerships to develop through the joint planning and teaching required. Finally, the awareness created by some projects had resulted in changes to the school's language policy, in curriculum or materials development, or in improved liaison between departments.

The future

Section 3 of the questionnaire asked participants for their thoughts on where their research might take them in the future. Five themes emerged: moving on to the next stage of the research cycle and basically 'doing more of the same'; tracking the language development of particular learners over a longer period of time; involving more staff in what they were doing i.e. disseminating their work in some way; adjusting their research focus – refining it, making it 'more systematic', or, interestingly, loosening its structure; and following up or replicating what another group had done.

Some Reflections

From the perspective of the University

The LEAP Research Project represented for the University a distinct shift in role from supplier of input to facilitator of research. The input role itself had a number of features which for us made it a potentially more effective in-service model than others we had experienced. These features continued to apply in the research phase.

First, it had brought us four years of unbroken contact with the same group of teachers, helping to build up mutual trust and understanding, and a deepening knowledge of each other's work. Second, the fact that the LEAP management were buying in the university to work with the whole language support team meant that 'we went to them' as opposed to the teachers 'coming to us', perhaps the more typical in-service practice. This is not a trivial point. In-service input provided on the teachers' own territory increases the likelihood that the content is made relevant to their concerns. The third feature is linked to the second. The LEAP service chose the CELSE modules which they felt to be most relevant to the needs of the support staff. In that sense, to use the language of the market place, they were buying an existing product. The challenge for the tutors, therefore, was to 'customise' the content without surrendering what they considered to be key academic components of the module. The fourth feature underpinned the other three. This was the respect that the LEAP management team clearly had for 'theory'. University tutors felt able to share their knowledge, confident that they had the support of the management team in valuing its importance, and also that it would be followed up in future management-led sessions.

The change in role, then, represented a mutually held belief by CELSE and LEAP staff that this autonomous capacity on the part of the teachers to combine received and experiential knowledge should be exploited by providing them with a framework within which to conduct their own research. Apart from the role of provider of input, the other role traditionally associated with university tutors is that of someone who 'does research on' pupils, teachers, schools and so on. Despite being a role that has been fundamentally criticised in recent years, because of its tendency to exacerbate the gulf between universities and schools and because of its failure to influence practice (Somekh, 1993, for example, is one of many to make this point), there is a sense in which recent government policy to relate funding in higher education to research output (through the Research Assessment Exercise) may be said to have inhibited this renegotiation of traditional research roles. However, CELSE and LEAP were both convinced of the value of, and need for, this new phase of co-operation and were in agreement that, after the initial input on action research, the role of the university staff should be that of 'facilitator', 'advisor', 'consultant', 'critical friend'.

From the perspective of the Support Service

The fifteen projects involving over forty teachers introduced the Service's staff to aspects of research methodology that will enable them to analyse their teaching in a more rigorous and authoritative way, thereby improving the quality of provision for all pupils. Participating schools valued the status that the research project brought them. Through projects like this, we aim to see an improvement in the status and value of EAL work on a national level. For that reason we gave a fuller version of this paper (see Beaumont *et al*, 1998) in January 1998 at the International Congress for School Effectiveness and Improvement, hoping to contribute in some way to the growing research base in the field of EAL, as well as persuading a wider professional audience of the value of collaboration between EAL staff, mainstream teachers, and teacher educators in the HE sector.

Postscript

Recent changes to government funding appear to be in serious danger of disrupting the kind of professional and coherent support to bilingual pupils provided by services such as LEAP, and of undermining attempts to improve classroom practice such as those described in this paper. For a full discussion of these changes and their implications, see Jones (1999).

Acknowledgements

We wish to make it clear that, as the authors of this paper, we simply represent the many who were involved in the Project. The credit for any success it enjoyed therefore goes to: primarily, all the support teachers, mainstream teachers, and pupils involved in the fifteen projects; the other members of the LEAP management team – Gail Newnham and Linda Sandler – and the Resource Centre staff; the two other CELSE tutors – Jane Andrews and Teresa O'Brien; and the staff of the University of Manchester Media Centre.

References

Allwright, D. (1993) Integrating 'research' and 'pedagogy': appropriate criteria and practical possibilities. In Edge and Richards (Eds) pp 125-135.

Beaumont, M., Coates, M. and Turrell, J. (1998) Language Support and School Effectiveness: A team-based approach to practitioner research. *Proceedings of the 11th International Congress for School Effectiveness and Improvement (ICSEI 98)*. University of Manchester: School of Education.

Bourne, J. (1989) *Moving into the Mainstream: LEA Provision for Bilingual Pupils*. Windsor: NFER/Nelson.

Cohen, L. and L. Manion (1994) *Research Methods in Education*. London: Routledge and Kegan Paul.

Edge, J. and Richards, K. (Eds, 1993) *Teachers Develop Teachers Research: Papers on classroom research and teacher development*. Oxford: Heinemann.

Elliott, J. (1991) *Action Research for Educational Change*. Milton Keynes: Open University Press.

Hopkins, D. (1985) *A Teacher's Guide to Classroom Research.* Milton Keynes: Open University Press.

Jones, I. (1999) EAL – Into the Millennium or Back to the Broom Cupboard? Watford: *NALDIC Newsletter* 19.

Leung, C. (1996) Linguistic Diversity in the 1990s: Some Language Education Issues for Minority Ethnic Pupils. Watford: *NALDIC Occasional Paper* 7.

Somekh, B. (1993) Quality in educational research – the contribution of classroom teachers. In Edge and Richards (Eds) pp 26-38.

Note

LEAP is funded by the LEA with support from central government via Section 11 of the Local Government Act of 1966. It co-ordinates 72 staff in all: 52 language support teachers, eleven bilingual assistants, and three bilingual clerks working in teams in 24 nursery, primary and secondary schools administered by the authority. Schools with large numbers of bilingual pupils may have five or more support staff working permanently on the premises. Other schools have smaller teams and a few schools have a part-time input. LEAP's central resource centre carries a management team of three and three administrative/resource staff. The management team co-ordinates a weekly half day meeting of all the teaching staff. The Resource Centre comprises a library, a bank of teacher-produced materials, a publishing base and other reprographic and technical equipment. The team provides language support for, evaluates and records the individual language development and monitors the progress of, more than 5000 bilingual pupils across the authority, a number which has more than doubled since 1980. Support staff also run in-service workshops for mainstream teachers in schools and for other LEAs, raising awareness of issues relating to the background and teaching of bilingual pupils.

CHAPTER TWO

Researching the use of ideational frameworks to support bilingual pupils' oracy and literacy skills in mainstream primary classrooms

Jane Andrews
University of Manchester

Fiona Fogarty
Sparrow Hill Primary School, Rochdale

Introduction

At the time of writing, the National Literacy Strategy (NLS) and the Literacy Hour (LH) are in their first year of operation and discussions of how teachers support bilingual pupils' oracy and literacy skills in the mainstream tend to be dominated by the terminology and approaches set down. The project presented here reflects the concerns about bilingual learners' oracy and literacy development and the initiatives taken by a team of primary language support teachers from Sparrow Hill School in Rochdale before the NLS began. The project is outlined from the perspectives of the Language for Educational Access Project (LEAP) teacher (FF) and a university-based 'critical friend' (JA). Their reflections on how what has been learnt may feed into future literacy work with bilingual pupils are presented at the end.

The project was carried out by four language support teachers eager to make links between the input encountered in various INSET training courses and their own practice in Key Stages 1 and 2 in a school with 402 pupils in total, of whom 362 use English as an additional language. Of the EAL pupils, 252 speak Punjabi/Mirpuri, 77 Urdu, 28 Sylheti/Bengali, two Kuchi, one Gujurati, one Swahili and one German. The trigger for the project is explained below in an extract from a report produced at the end of the initial cycle of research activity by FF, the co-ordinator of the LEAP team at the school:

> We had been receiving some excellent in-service training from the University course, from Pat McEldowney and from colleagues at LEAP. However, we did not feel that we had been able to incorporate many of the good ideas into our own practice. Much of the material was aimed most obviously at KS2 whereas most of our support is targeted at KS1 and the early years. Although we realised it was perfectly possible to adapt many of the ideas to suit younger pupils, we simply had not had the time to do this. The research project offered not only the occasion to adapt the materials but further gave us the rare chance to do this as a team.

This quotation reflects the spirit in which the project was carried out, that is, a collaborative approach to the implementation of ideas encountered in INSET.

Background to the Research Area

Following the scheme for 'exploratory teaching' described in Chapter One, the four LEAP teachers set about defining the topic they wanted to focus on in their research. They wanted to explore the practice of using 'frameworks' for supporting bilingual pupils' speech and writing. The teachers were stimulated by input presented in training sessions which promoted the principle of supporting pupils' productive use of language through the use of 'ideational frameworks' (Burgess, 1994 and Chapter 12 of this book) as they engage with tasks which are part of a 'language learning cycle' (McEldowney, 1982). Figure 1 presents the general way in which a framework might be integrated into oracy and literacy work to serve a supportive function.

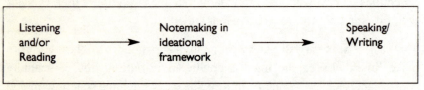

Figure 1 (taken from Burgess and Carter 1996)

An example of how a framework might be used is outlined in Figure 2 to illustrate the nature of the input the team received during INSET.

1.	Pupils listen to or read about some new information.
2.	Pupils make notes into an ideational framework (a table, flow diagram or tree diagram) which helps them to organise and conceptualise the information.
3.	Pupils use notes made in the ideational framework to speak about the information and/or to write about it. The content and organisation of the notes support pupils' language production (written or spoken).

Figure 2: How the framework is used.

As part of the exploratory teaching described in this chapter, LEAP teachers adapted the model illustrated in Figure 1 to suit the needs of their bilingual pupils.

The Research Focus

As well as defining the general area of interest outlined above, the LEAP teachers also identified a specific research focus. This was described by FF as follows:

> We wanted to investigate ways of helping our pupils improve the standard of their oral and written output in English. As a team we often support our pupils as they are engaged in practical, first-hand experiences and were particularly interested in supporting their reporting back to others of these.

The team planned to build on their existing practice of ensuring that all pupils are supported in their participation in curriculum-based activities. The rationale for the specific research focus was developed further as the group worked through the early stages of Allwright's scheme; this development is shown in the following quotation from FF:

> At KS2 we are already using DARTS techniques to good effect and frameworks complement that approach. They also seemed to offer the opportunity to tightly control the verbal output of pupils which seemed an interesting and possibly balancing alternative to the more general influence we effected in our Structured Play Areas (a favoured technique in our Early Years).

The benefits of using play as a teaching and learning technique are well documented in the primary school literature (eg. Moyles, 1994, Hall and

Robinson, 1995). Play has been noted as valuable in helping pupils' development of oracy and literacy skills. The normal practice during structured play sessions was to encourage pupils to respond to their experiences using the language at their disposal at the time. That is to say, no structured language teaching was used as part of the structured play session. FF wanted to find out how well ideational frameworks fitted into the scheme of structured play.

The Allwright procedure encouraged all of the LEAP teachers to move on from this general stage of thinking to list a research question and some subsidiary questions as a way of becoming familiar with the topic area. The questions produced were:

Main question

Can pupils retrieve the information on the framework and use it to support their own speech and writing?

Subsidiary questions

1. Will the use of frameworks raise standards?

2. Can frameworks be adapted to suit different age and ability groups?

3. Will the framework structure create over-dependency?

4. How will we wean pupils off the supportive framework structure?

5. Will pupils be able to use the vocabulary/sentence structure of the framework at a later date/without its presence?

6. How long-lasting a support will a framework provide?

The questions indicate that the teachers engaged in the research project with a genuine sense of critical inquiry; they wanted to find out what the boundaries of this teaching strategy would be and what effects it would have on EAL pupils' productive language skills. It is clear now that some of the questions (1,4,6) imply a longitudinal approach and others (2, 3, 5 and the main question) could be explored during a shorter period. The extent to which the research addressed these questions will be revisited at the end of the chapter.

Procedure and materials

With these questions in mind, the LEAP teachers planned their classroom and data collection procedures. Allwright (1993) advocates that classroom research should make use of familiar procedures as a way of ensuring that the research or 'exploratory teaching' is manageable and non-intrusive. (This is in contrast with the use of more traditional research instruments, such as formal questionnaires, which may not feature in day to day classroom activities.) The teachers were attracted to the concept of using familiar procedures as this created little increase in workload at a time when the school was to undergo an OfSTED inspection.

The research was planned in the following way:

> We decided to opt for LEAP teachers to work with small groups of pupils maybe on firsthand experiences or at least making reference to real objects. Teachers or pupils would then fill in relevant information on a framework. Pupils would then use the framework to support an oral or written report. The framework could then remain *in situ* for further use by pupils eg. in the structured play area. (FF)

The teachers planned to monitor their work using frameworks with different groups of pupils in a variety of ways. Firstly, lesson plans would serve to describe the activity in which the frameworks would be used. Secondly, as teachers were already used to completing language analysis sheets as part of their collaborative lesson planning with mainstream teachers, it was agreed that these would provide useful instruments for comparing pupils' production of spoken and written language with their teachers' planned lesson focus. An evaluation sheet was also designed on which LEAP teachers could record their comments about the lesson in which frameworks were used. Finally, pupils' written and spoken production would be captured on paper and on video. Data gathered using these monitoring procedures are presented below.

Data

The pupils using EAL in the two reception classes at the time of the research were all within the first three stages of the five LEAP stages of assessment. The teacher's pre-lesson planning included a 'Language Analysis and Focus' sheet (see Figure 3).

Language for Educational Access Project	
Language Analysis and Focus	
Curriculum Area	English
Activity	using a framework for goods bought on the market and follow-up individual worksheets
Core Language Activity	
Language Structures	'X bought some ...eg apples'; 'Can I have...'; 'I want some ...' at SPA (Structured Play Area)
Particular Features	bought – irregular past tense – some pupils usually say 'buyed'; I might expect 'I buyed a apple'
Vocabulary	some flowers, some apples, some bananas, some oranges, some strawberries, some carrots; shopkeeper, customer
Particular Features	NB all items plural names of people in group
Principle Functions	label and identity; report in past tense; asking for goods; greetings; leave taking; 'goodbye', 'thank you'
Teacher Talk	give instructions; establish framework and their own worksheet
Pupil Talk	SPA – 'Can I have...?' 'I want some...' rehearsing specific sentence structure of framework, asking for clarification re task, 'reading' eg names
Reading Tasks	their own and other's names; 'read' back from framework and their own worksheet
Writing Tasks	complete worksheet by writing names or cutting and sticking them in appropriate place

Figure 3: Language Analysis Sheet

Observational data relating to the lesson in action is presented through the eyes of JA, with selected illustrative quotations from the teacher's and pupils' output.

Fieldnotes from university-based observer:
Stages of Session

Stage 1

The Structured Play Task is set by the teacher.

Pupils mingle with 'shopkeepers' and 'buy' the appropriate fruit and vegetables (plaster models which pupils have been involved in making in a previous lesson). Pupils talk about their play with the teacher:

A   he give me some money – I give it back to him!

FF   did you ask him what you wanted?

A   yes

FF   and have you got what you wanted S?

S   I want 3 [inaudible]

Stages 2 and 3

A reporting back session – pupils joined their teacher sitting in a circle and were encouraged to talk about what they had 'bought' with the teacher's invitation 'we're going to have a look at all these lovely things you've bought,' indicating a large basket which contained all the items. Individual pupils answer the teacher's questions (eg. what are these things? what did you buy? who bought the flowers?). Pupils use a combination of single word utterances ('me', 'carrots', 'David') in answer to specific questions from the teacher as well as longer spontaneous utterances ('yum! they're all hard now!' as a comment on the fact that the plaster has set and made the fruit and vegetables solid; 'all of them out!' as a pupil takes out all of one type of fruit/vegetable from the basket).

Stage 4

Using the framework: the teacher sets up a text creation activity using cards (jumbled up on the floor) which are colour-coded (yellow for pupils' names, green for verb form 'bought', blue for pictures of fruit and vegetables). Pupils are invited to select appropriate cards to create a simple sentence about what they bought eg. 'Humma bought some strawberries'. 'David bought some carrots'. etc.; the cards are stuck to a magnet board and the set of sentences builds up. Each pupil creates her/his own sentence according to what they bought during the structured play until a complete set of sentences is on the board. Pupils help each other to select the appropriate cards and there is a lot of rehearsal of words and phrases during this time (eg. 'some carrots ... no! some strawberries').

The group and then individuals are encouraged to read the sentences from the board using the picture and word prompts. Board work – reporting back using mixture of visuals and words on cards 'reading' names, item bought. The teacher encourages volunteers to attempt to read out the full set of sentences. Once again a lot of rehearsal is going on in the background as the volunteers read the sentences.

To illustrate the nature of the framework used in the lesson, the cards used by pupils to build up personalised sentences about their shopping are presented in Figure 4 below.

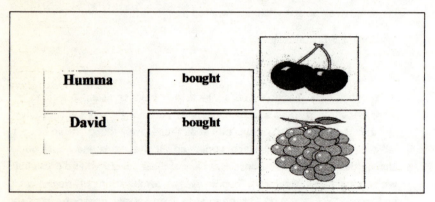

Figure 4: Framework following structured play based on buying goods in the market.

Analysis and Reflections

To reflect on the process and outcomes of the research project, we now return to the original research questions. The main question (Can pupils retrieve the information on the framework and use it to support their own speech and writing?) relates to the suitability of the teaching technique to the needs of the pupils. From the observer's notes it is clear that the framework provided a focus for pupils reporting back on what they had bought. The technique was used with individual pupils who 'created' a sentence about their own experience with the help of the colour-coded cards. The technique also provided a focus for literacy work with the whole group, who were engaged in rehearsing the language, as individuals searched for the appropriate cards for their experience.

So the answer to the main research question is yes, the pupils were able to support their oracy and literacy using the framework. Let us now look at the subsidiary questions capable of being answered in the short term.

Subsidiary questions:

- Can frameworks be adapted to suit different age and ability groups?

- Will the framework structure create over-dependency?

- Will pupils be able to use the vocabulary/sentence structure of the framework at a later date/without it?

The question of the adaptability of the frameworks was explored by the four LEAP teachers as they incorporated ideational frameworks into their teaching in various curriculum areas across the school. A comment by FF indicates how mainstream teachers received this new way of working:

> Although we had not devised an objective measure for assessing the success of frameworks, our previous experience told us we were making advances with this method. Also a telling sign was that before we had decided to share our findings with mainstream colleagues they began to ask. They had been impressed by the confidence of pupils reporting back and they began to use our framework materials and then to devise their own.

This point is elaborated below with details of how differentiated outcomes were achieved following structured language work with a framework:

> From being concerned about their [the frameworks'] seemingly restricted nature we in fact found them very suitable for adapting to suit the skills and needs of individuals. For instance, having produced a set of resources and gone over the basic framework with a group it was easy to ask pupils to respond in different ways; an able reader in reception could go on to produce his or her own sentences based on the framework whereas a less confident pupil could reproduce the sentences on the framework (or slight variants) by matching or arranging prepared words on colour coded card. Older pupils with varying levels of competence in English could be directed to fill in appropriate elements of a framework while all feeling they had contributed to the whole. (FF)

Additional benefits were also noted by teachers regarding their own work, as indicated below:

...in preparing framework materials at whatever level you cannot lose sight of the complexities of the language demands being made of the pupils.

Another 'short term' subsidiary research question related to whether pupils would be able to use the vocabulary or sentence structure of the framework at a later date without its presence. Teachers gave some answers to this during the follow-up to lessons which involved the use of frameworks. The language output from all pupils (both emerging bilinguals and monolingual speakers of English) was noted to have been enriched as a result of the lesson. In particular, teachers noticed that when particular language forms were focused on via a framework, pupils were more likely to use the structure in their own speech and writing at a later date. In response to this observation, LEAP teachers adopted the strategy of leaving the materials from the framework (in this case the coloured cards) in the structured play area so that pupils could incorporate them into their play.

As stated earlier, the LEAP teachers involved in the project were ready to identify any weaknesses in the strategy. For instance, there were concerns about the risk of pupils' use of language being restricted by their using a framework. One of the subsidiary research questions addressed the issue of whether frameworks would create an overdependency in pupils when reporting back to the class. On reflection the LEAP teachers considered that these concerns were unjustified. It seems that the frameworks allowed for flexibility in terms of how teachers and pupils worked, as well as providing support for pupils who needed it. As FF remarked:

> We would not advocate an unnatural diet of clipped sentences but [we noticed that] tight structure and a measured control of pupils' use of language has enabled them to succeed.

The main focus of the LEAP teacher's function is facilitating curriculum access for EAL pupils and promoting achievement and this is clearly being facilitated by the use of frameworks.

A model for using ideational frameworks in early years classes

The way in which the framework was used in the lesson outlined above differed from the typical approach taken by the teacher in a structured play session. We can see how the approach sketched out in Figures 1 and 2 has been adapted. The language at the reporting-back stage is tightly controlled so that pupils are guided in their use of just one verb form (in this case the irregular form 'bought') in the context of a simple sentence.

Support for pupils in their use of language is also provided by colour coding on the prompt cards attached to the magnetic board as part of the framework. The colour coding encourages pupils to see patterns in the language forms they are using for particular purposes (eg. names come at the beginning of a phrase when reporting back in this way). The magnet board is also used for language support, allowing pupils to see how sentences and phrases are built from patterns of words.

Some differences between the 'at the market' structured play session and the 'framework-based' activities outlined in Figure 2 relate largely to the way in which the framework is used. In the structured play session, the details of the framework are not 'created' by the pupils in the way that the notes are created by pupils in Figure 2. But, the structure of the framework is created by the pupils while they report back on what they have bought. In this sense the framework is personalised and so has a motivating effect.

In the light of the exploratory teaching, we can represent the use of ideational frameworks within a structured play context in the following way (updating the Burgess and Carter, 1996 model in Figure 1).

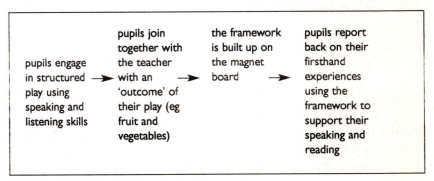

Figure 5: Ideational framework for structured play.

Frameworks, the NLS and the future

Conclusions about the research project drawn in 1997 need to be re-visited in the light of current practice and debate. When the NLS materials were first published (DfEE, 1998a), there was concern among language support staff about the absence of reference to EAL pupils' needs. Additional guidelines (DfEE, 1998b) have since been produced which make some reference to EAL pupils' needs but at a very general level.

For the LEAP teachers who participated in the classroom research project, the desire to initiate a whole-school implementation of various uses of frameworks has been put on hold due to the introduction of the NLS. However, an overlap between the focused language work enshrined in the framework approach and the NLS has been noted. The current feeling is that once the NLS has been worked through in its entirety, teachers may feel ready to bring more of their own experience and expertise to bear on literacy work for EAL pupils. When this stage arrives, LEAP teachers feel they can develop the use of frameworks and also follow up some of the more long-term subsidiary research questions noted earlier in this chapter.

Several more general issues emerged from this research project which are worth noting here. Firstly, the classroom research structure provided a valuable way of guiding teachers in their exploration and adaptation of ideas encountered during INSET which did not immediately appear applicable to their teaching context. Secondly, the success of the classroom research project appeared to owe much to the fact that teachers worked as a team to plan, implement, report on and evaluate their work. Finally, the benefits of focusing on language form within traditional learning contexts in primary classrooms, for example, structured play, was seen to benefit bilingual pupils and monolingual pupils alike.

References

Allwright, D. (1993) Integrating 'research' and 'pedagogy': appropriate criteria and practical possibilities. In Edge, J. and Richards, K. (Eds) *Teachers Develop Teachers Research*. Oxford: Heinemann pp 125-135.

Burgess, J. (1994) Ideational frameworks in integrated language learning. *System* 22/3: 309-318.

Burgess, J. and Carter, I. (1996) Common codes for mainstream ESL support across the curriculum. *System* 24/2: 211-222.

Davies, F. (1995) *Introducing Reading*. Harmondsworth: Penguin.

Department for Education and Employment (1998a) *The National Literacy Strategy – Framework for Teaching*. London: DfEE.

DfEE (1998b) *The National Literacy Strategy – Additional Guidance*. London: DfEE.

Hall , N. and Robinson, A. (1995) *Exploring Writing and Play in the Early Years*. London: David Fulton.

Moyles, J. (Ed, 1994) *The Excellence of Play*. Milton Keynes: Open University.

McEldowney, P. M . (1982) *English in Context – Teacher's book*. Sunbury on Thames: Nelson.

Note

1. Directed Activities Related to Texts (Davies, 1995).

CHAPTER THREE

Input and output in primary science: a case study

Teresa O'Brien
University of Manchester

Gail Newnham
Language for Educational Access Project, Rochdale

Lynn Tinker
Belfield Community School, Rochdale

Introduction

This chapter tells the story of a group taking part in the in-service programme described in Chapter One. The group was rather different from the others as it included one primary language support teacher (Lynn Tinker) and the LEAP Primary Team Co-ordinator (Gail Newnham); other teams included only language support teachers. While the first-named author is the main narrator of this text, the voices of Gail (GN) and Lynn (LT) will be heard as I draw from the reports they wrote on completion of their research cycles and from discussions we had during the creation of this paper. The stages of the project structure the chapter.

Identifying a puzzle area and formulating a question

From the outset, the LEAP service intended that the work carried out during the project would be consistent with their long-term educational aims. GN wrote:

> It was felt that the focus of the Primary Action Research Projects in Nursery and at Key Stage I should relate to supporting access and acquisition through the development of oracy. At Key Stage 2, the chosen focus was the integration of the four language skills, highlighting the importance of the role of oracy.

As Primary Team Co-ordinator, GN did not have a classroom teaching role but as she wanted to be fully involved in the research work, she approached LT. With the approval of the Headteacher, they began the research process together. GN wrote:

> We began by thinking about how we, as teachers of English as an Additional Language (EAL), plan for oracy. All Primary LEAP staff complete a planning sheet entitled 'Language Analysis and Focus'. This is routinely used to analyse the language of a particular activity as part of the planning process. It enables LEAP staff to predict the possible language content of any curriculum-based activity with reference to language structures, vocabulary, functions, teacher talk, pupil talk and literacy tasks. **However, as far as we knew, no-one had ever tested out whether the language predicted was actually used in the ensuing lesson. Lynn and I decided to assess the effectiveness of the document by attempting to correlate the language used with the language predicted.**

LT and GN did not start from a pedagogical problem but from a wish to know whether the procedures advocated by the LEAP team really were effective. Successfully pursued, the investigation might lead to findings of relevance to the whole team and to all language support teachers. This was how they formulated their question:

> Does the language predicted by the teacher (the language focus sheet) correlate with the actual language outcomes (the language produced by the children)?

Brainstorming answers and listing subsidiary questions

During this stage, LT and GN suggested that the correlation between language input and language output would vary according to *the subject being studied, the nature of the group, the 'oral climate' the expertise of the teacher, the technical nature of the language and the personalities of the children.* Implicitly they acknowledged that their question was not a simple one and that their first attempt to fill the gap in their knowledge would need to be followed up in various ways. Formulating subsidiary questions proved to be quite difficult. Looking back on the questions, we now agree that they did not really perform the refining function intended by Allwright (1993). Possible questions might have dealt with the amount of repetition in teacher input, the role of monolingual children as linguistic models, and whether output in written form was to be as valued as output in oral form.

Writing a more focused question

LT and GN further focused their question by deciding on a particular curriculum area:

> Does the language predicted by the teacher (the language focus planning sheet) correlate with the actual language outcomes (the language produced by the children) in different Science activities on either light or sound with a Year 3 class?

They chose a primary science session based on string telephones for the pilot study as science offered good opportunities for activity-based learning and integrated skills work.

Outlining in detail the classroom procedures to be used for the exploration

Allwright (1993) advocates the use of well-tried classroom activities as the focus of exploration. LT and GN worked in the way LT and the mainstream teacher normally did, but this time LT took the role of the mainstream teacher, and GN that of the support teacher. They planned a session involving discussion, experiment and post-experiment discussion. They would share the teaching and the videotaping they were to use for record-keeping. They worked to the curriculum requirement that

> Pupils should learn that sounds are heard because they travel to the ear and that they do so via a variety of materials. Sounds cause vibrations.

Following usual practice, the teachers produced a language focus sheet for the first session. (Figure 1 gives an example for a later lesson).

The subjects were four bilingual learners in a mixed ability group of nine Year 3 pupils. This group was extracted from the main class in order to sharpen the focus of the project and to facilitate filming. Three of the bilingual learners (referred to here as EAL children) had attended the school from the nursery stage, and the fourth from reception stage. All four had benefited from language support throughout their schooling and at the time of the project were supported for one afternoon per week by LT within the mainstream class. The remaining children, referred to as 'linguistic models' (LM), had been at the school since the reception stage and were all monolingual English speakers. LEAP tutors work on the assumption that bilingual children will learn by sharing an activity with others who are in some way more knowledgeable (cf Leung and Cable, 1997:34).

Identifying suitable data collection procedures and piloting the procedures with a small group of students

Allwright has expressed concern about the time and energy needed for teachers to feel confident with data collection and monitoring procedures (1997:368). LT and GN had decided to videotape their class and transcribe the resulting record in order to analyse it. The lesson took place around a table before and after a practical session during which the children experimented with the string telephones. There were difficulties, however. GN wrote:

> During this activity we had planned to share the teaching role by using the camcorder attached to the tripod, which would have allowed us the freedom to do that. However, we quickly realised that this would be very difficult, as the basic camcorder and tripod did not allow the children or ourselves enough freedom of movement. This ability to move and, more importantly, to be clearly heard for the purpose of the subsequent tape transcription meant that we had to change plans. LT took the role of teacher and I took on the role of camcorder operator and observer.

Nevertheless, a videotaped record was produced which allowed LT to transcribe the parts of the lesson which took place around the table.

Making any necessary alterations or improvements

Looking back, we recognise that the piloting exercise mainly focused on the videotaping and transcription. The research question relating to language input and output was not really addressed although a certain amount of data analysis was carried out. This was, however, evaluative rather than descriptive and was done with the aid of the report sheets normally used for the analysis of written work and oral discourse as part of a student monitoring system. I could not be present at this pilot stage but was given an oral report at one of the in-service afternoons. The main points communicated at this stage were:

- it had not been possible for both teachers to take part in the lesson as planned because of the need for one of them to look after the camera

- LT felt that the lesson had gone as planned but had been worried that the noise from an overhead heater had interfered with the sound quality

- they had both been delighted when one of the EAL children had used an onomatopoeic verb to describe the noise he had heard (zizzled – not a word that had been predicted!)

Apart from the report sheets, no analysis of the data was carried out. LT notes honestly *'we decided that we needed more (or better) data to work with or perhaps we were just reluctant to get down to the evaluation of the data we already had'*.

The part-time nature of CELSE's involvement and the fact that I was facilitating other groups meant that I was not able to follow this up, so the project continued with no particular linguistic insights having been gained from the immense amount of work that had gone into transcribing. We have since looked at the data; the findings are discussed in a later section.

Fortunately, because CELSE and LEAP wanted official video-recordings of some of the projects, a professional crew was used to record the second session, and LT and GN were able to run it co-operatively. GN and LT prepared language analysis sheets independently. The different results can be seen in Figure 1 below.

A few differences emerge: GN seems to be more conscious of connectors and of the potential for use of the passive. She has also thought about pre-positional phrases (eg. in the cupboard). In the section on pupil talk, she seems more focused on the formal reporting of the experiment, leaning towards the written form, while LT seems to be thinking through the language that will be used in the oral discussion. In the skills box, again GN seems more interested in writing while LT focuses a little more on reading. In our reflective stage we decided that GN's need to generalise in her role as team co-ordinator and LT's deeper knowledge of the situation and the learners meant they did things differently.

LANGUAGE FOR EDUCATIONAL ACCESS PROJECT

LANGUAGE ANALYSIS AND FOCUS

	GN ANALYSIS	LT ANALYSIS
CURRICULUM AREA	Science AT1 Experimental and Investigative Science AT 2 Life Processes and Living Things	
ACTIVITY	Growing mustard and cress seeds Investigation of conditions needed for growth. Discussion of results. Sentence matching. Writing up results	Growth experiments 1) Recollection 2) discussion comparison 3) sentence matching 4) write up of results
LANGUAGE STRUCTURE	*CORE LANGUAGE OF ACTIVITY* Question forms: Use of did in questions. Simple past for description – put, grew. Use of connectives 'then', 'and', 'but', 'next'. Use of passive 'light is needed to make food to make plants grow'. Perfect tense – it has... Plants need... In order to grow. This one is... scientific present	Mix perfect and present tense – scientific present
VOCABULARY PARTICULAR FEATURE	Mustard, cress, seeds, cotton wool, food, plant, plastic trays, sugar, light, oxygen, carbon dioxide, dark, water, window ledge/ sill, cupboard, yellow, weak, tall, strong	Cupboard water grew experiment put yellow Cress place taller tray sleeve weaker cotton wool

Figure 1: Two pre-lesson language analyses

	healthy, green, leaf/leaves, this, that (range of adjectives). Why/because, prepositions – in the cupboard, on the window ledge, water, put, place(d) prepare(d), observe(d) grow, grew.	grow this seeds prepare that sugar carbon dioxide. Comparative adjectives – some specific scientific language.
PRINCIPAL FUNCTIONS	Labelling, describing, questioning, hypothesising explaining, reasoning	Relation of past events – reason – explanation – description – comparison – hypothesis
TEACHER TALK	What did we use? What did we do? What happened? Why did it happen? Description of investigation. Evaluation of results. When we grew cress seeds in a cupboard... on the window ledge/sill.	Can you remember? Why has it grown taller? Then what did we do? Today we are going to? What is the scientific word for... What do you think? What do plants need?
PUPIL TALK	Description of process of plants and investigation. Past tense	The cress is... This one is... This It's grown... er It's happened because...
READING TASKS		Reading what they wrote in previous lesson. Reading cloze passage.
WRITING TASKS	Use of formal framework for writing up an investigation. Title. Diagram. What we did. What happened. Why it happened. Integrated language skills model. Oracy/Literacy linked throughout.	Filling in cloze passage.

*Figure 1: Two pre-lesson language analyses (continued) *The LEAP teachers use Lewis and Wray 1997.*

Implementing the full study

We were able to triangulate the observation of the second session. The expert use of the video camera resulted in a very good recording; JA[1] completed an observation sheet prepared in advance by GN, and I took detailed field notes. Once the video recording had been transcribed, we had a very rich picture of what had occurred. The lesson had seven stages:

1   Recalling – 'Can you remember the experiment we did last week?'

2   Comparing – 'Now, today, we're going to look at these (trays of cress). Which one did we put in the cupboard?'

3   Drawing and writing – 'Up here we'd like you to do a picture of tray A – and you're going to do a picture here – a diagram of tray A ...'

4   Sentence-matching – 'What we've got here are lots of sentences...'

5   Hypothesising – 'Well what do you think? Do seeds need light to grow?'

6   Reading and writing – 'Right do you think you could write about what happened...'

7   Writing – hypothesising, 'Why did...?'

This time LT and GN took the research through to the analysis stage. They reported struggling for a long time over how to do this and eventually tackled it in different ways, producing a detailed view of the language output of the children. This is presented in the next section which is based on work done for their M.Ed assignments, for a presentation they gave to a local teachers' association and on further work done for this chapter.

Reporting on the Studies – Findings – Evaluation

What we later discovered from Study 1 (Lesson on sound)

First we can look at what we might have found had we had time to analyse the transcript of the lesson on sound. It did not cover the whole lesson but focused on the discussion sections before and after the experimental part. 253 turns were found: the T used 124 (49%) of these and the remainder were taken by the children as follows:

Ranking	Child	Status	No. of turns
1	J	LM	52
2	A	LM	21
3	F	EAL	19
4	C	LM	12
4	K	EAL	12
6	H	EAL	11
7	B	LM	10
8	Sa	LM	0

Table 1: Ranking of turns

The teachers could have predicted that J would take most turns. He is an unusually talkative child. If we extract the most and the least talkative, however, we see three well-balanced pairs.

As part of my contribution to the study, I analysed the transcript using *Wordsmith* (Scott, 1997). This allowed us to see how much of the predicted (and unpredicted) language was used and by whom. Only five of the predicted items (14.3%) did not appear at all in the lesson. Clearly, the correlation between predicted and used language was positive. When we looked at who was using the language we found that 68.3% of the items were produced by the teacher, giving a figure quite close to the two-thirds/ one third ratio often cited as typical of the division of classroom talk time. Although the LM children seemed to produce three times as many items as the EAL children, one child was responsible for a great deal of that variance as we saw in Table 1. Would we find something similar in the second study?

Study 2 findings

Again, GN and LT worked independently. GN divided her results into *Receptive* and *Productive*, and within the latter she looked at *speech* and *writing*. As the video showed all students listening attentively to the input, GN inferred that all students had 'received' the same input. She satisfied herself that all the target structures, vocabulary and functions had indeed been used by the teachers at least once.

She then looked at the productive output of the target children under the headings of *spoken* and *written*. She gave a point for each predicted item

Language item	Total no used	Teachers	EAL learners	Linguistic model learners	Both groups of learners
Cress	20	17	13	1	–
Seeds	56	28		15	
Cotton wool	6	5		–	
Food	25	14	8	3	–
Plant 2 plants 19	21	12	6	3	
Tray	66	36	20	9	
Light	72	32	20	20	
Dark	21	6	7	7	
Water	11	8	2	–	
Window sill	26	14	6	6	
Cupboard	35	19	11	4	
Yellow	17	6	7	4	
Weak	8	4	3	–	
Weaker	2	0	–	–	
Tall	–	–	0	0	
Taller	6	4	–	2	
Strong	7	5	–	–	
Stronger	–	0	–	–	
Healthy	36	23	9	4	
Unhealthy (not predicted)	5	–	3	–	

Table 2: Production of predicted items

Language item	Total no used	Teachers	EAL learners	Linguistic model learners	Both groups of learners
Green	20	12	3	5	
Leaf/leaves (only plural used)	7	3	3	1	
Sugar	1	0	1	0	
Carbon dioxide	5	3	2	0	
Oxygen	3	1	0	1	—
Why	12	12	0	0	
Because	22	10	10	3	
'cos	7	1	1	5	
Experiment	6	6	0	0	
Put	31	23	3	5	
Observe(d)	4	3	1	0	
Grow	17	11	2	4	
Grew	5	5	0	0	
Grown	13	9 (1 passive)	0	4	
Then	7	7	0	0	
But	12	11	0	1	
Next	3	3	0	0	
Total	**615 100%**	**355 58%**	**143 23%**	**114 18.6%**	**3 0.4%**

Table 2: Production of predicted items (continued)

produced. (Her analysis did not therefore take account of how many times the children produced the item or whether they produced it as a response or as part of an initiation.) She also noted the language functions (eg. *labelling, describing*) that had been realised in both teacher input and pupil output. Again, a point was given for each function realised. GN concluded that there was a positive correlation between predicted language items and used language items. However, most of the predicted items were found in the children's *written* output which had been in some ways guided by the teachers.

LT's analysis was different but complementary. She examined each of the 142 pupil turns to determine its function, and whether it was self-initiated, a voluntary response or a directed response (where the teacher had directed a question to a particular pupil). She also noted whether the structure was used correctly, whether the language had been predicted, and any non-predicted functions of language used. All the pupils were included in LT's analysis. The contributions of each child in each section of the lesson were categorised as *comparing, describing, explaining, hypothesising, labelling, recalling or other*. The *other* categories included *responding yes* or *no, informing, instructing*, and *clarifying*.

The analysis showed that from the point of view of vocabulary (LT and GN's lists had been almost identical) 30 of the predicted 34 items occurred in the oral parts of the lesson (including times when children were reading aloud). Thus, 88% of the items predicted were used in the lesson (cf 85.7% in study 1). But used by whom? Further analysis with *Wordsmith* led to the findings in Table 2.

Here is clear evidence that while, unsurprisingly, the teachers produced the majority of the selected items[2], the children between them produced 42%, and the emerging bilinguals actually produced slightly more of these items than the monolingual children. An important difference between the two lessons was the inclusion of reading and writing in lesson 2. Some of these instances were produced while children were reading aloud, and can be seen perhaps as constituting language practice only at a phonological level. However, we would argue that the very practical and visual nature of the earlier part of the lesson meant that the children were using the words meaningfully.

Functions	EAL children					Linguistic model children				
	H	K	Sh	F	Total	A	B	Sa	J	Total
Recalling	1	1		1	3	2			2	4
Describing	11	3		2	16	1			4	5
Explaining	3		1		4		2		4	6
Comparing		1	1	2	4	1	4		9	14
Hypothesising		1	2	1	4	1	2		3	6
Labelling	1	1		3	5	1			3	4
Questioning									2	2
Socialising									10	10
Other	5		2	2	9	1	1		17	19
Total	21	7	6	11	43	7	9	0	54	70
Reading	1	4	1	6	12	2	2	5	2	11
Total incl. Reading	22	11	7	17	57	9	11	5	56	81

Table 3: Instances of use of functions by individual children

I also performed a functional analysis, agreeing with LT in 90% of cases. I separated out pieces of language which were read aloud, so focused on the pupils' own output within the interactive parts of the class. Table 3 shows how each learner contributed to or participated in the lesson. We note that all eight were involved in reading. The teacher made sure that students who had been rather quiet in other parts of the lesson and who were perhaps less confident made a contribution. Accordingly, Sa read more than the other linguistic models.

Looking at the children's individual contributions, we see that the four bilingual learners all made contributions using a variety of functions. Although the total for the LM children is higher (54), there is great variation in the individual children's contributions owing to J's dominance. He is the only one who makes a social contribution. In contrast, Sa, apart from reading aloud, participated again mainly silently in the lesson. By now we felt that we had found many interesting answers to our question and ways in which the question could be pursued.

What we learnt from our findings and later reflection

Firstly, we realised that LT and GN, in seeking to focus their research, had produced conditions which were much better than could be found in a mainstream class. They had earlier suggested that the correlation between language input and the children's language output would vary according to the subject studied, the nature of the group, the 'oral climate', and the expertise of the teacher. This enabled us to put the findings in perspective. There was a need for a follow-up study which answered the question 'Does the experience recorded in this group approximate to the experience of children in a class led by a mainstream teacher?' Several American studies have reported that mainstream teachers are less likely to elicit output from bilingual students (Harklau, 1994). The data collected here could serve as a benchmark for further investigation in mainstream classes.

Reflection on the amount of productive language resulting from the children's writing induced thoughts about the guided nature of the lesson. Interest in the input-output dimension had led to focus on teacher-pupil interaction and the presence of two teachers in a small group had left little opportunity for pupil-pupil interaction. We reflected on the difference between the two lessons. The first had involved the children in experimentation and therefore included pupil-pupil talk. In the second, the pair-work was often facilitated by the teachers. There is obviously scope for more investigation of the relationship between spoken and written output.

Methodologically, GN and LT had practised transcription, discovering how time-consuming and difficult it was. They had also worked out their own analytic frameworks. LT had struggled with the difficulties of categorising functions and experienced the phenomenon of language with overlapping functions. She had also puzzled over the issue of data-driven versus inquiry-driven analysis. Although their question was a clear one, she had experienced the pull of the data as the transcript showed her things she had not thought about before. Allwright (1997) worries about asking hard-pressed teachers to spend time on research techniques which they do not have time to master completely. We all felt that the reflection stage, which included writing this chapter, helped us to reap the full value of our experiences and left us wanting to continue this type of enquiry.

References

Allwright, D. (1993) Integrating 'research' and 'pedagogy': appropriate criteria and practical possibilities. In Edge, J. and Richards, K. (Eds, 1993) *Teachers Develop Teachers Research*. Oxford: Heinemann.

Allwright, D. (1997) Quality and sustainability in teacher research. *TESOL Quarterly* 31/2: 368-370.

Edwards, D. and Mercer, N. (1995) *Common Knowledge: The Development of Understanding in the Classroom*. London: Routledge.

Harklau, L. (1994) ESL versus mainstream classes: contrasting L2 learning environments. *TESOL Quarterly* 28/2: 241-272.

Leung, C. and Cable, C. (Eds, 1997) *English as an Additional Language*. Watford: NALDIC (National Association for Language Development in the Curriculum).

Lewis, M. and Wray, D. (1997) *Writing Frames*. The Reading and Language Centre, University of Reading.

Scott, M. (1997) *Wordsmith*. Oxford: Oxford University Press.

Notes

1. Jane Andrews, a Manchester colleague (see Chapter 2)
2. It is worth noting that the figure of 58% falls considerably below the figure of 66% that we might expect if the 'two thirds rule' (Edwards and Mercer, 1995: 25) had been in operation.

CHAPTER FOUR

Putting discourse analysis theory into practice in the secondary English classroom: a fairy tale?

Julia Turrell
Language for Educational Access Project, Rochdale

Mike Beaumont
University of Manchester

Introduction

This chapter describes one of the research projects carried out as part of the one year in-service programme outlined in Chapter 1. It is written by the member of the university team who acted as facilitator to the research group (Mike Beaumont) and one of the language support teachers at Falinge Park High School (Julia Turrell) who taught the six lessons described. The target group was a class of twenty-seven Year 7 pupils in a large multi-ethnic secondary school in Rochdale in the North-West of England. Also present for the whole sequence of lessons was the mainstream English teacher of the class. Lesson 2, the main focus of the research, was attended by the university facilitator and by another member of the research group, who carried out the observation task.

The Planning Phase

The aim of the project was to put into classroom practice aspects of discourse analysis theory covered in a 30 hour INSET course previously delivered by Mike Beaumont and to evaluate their effectiveness. Following the revised form of Allwright's (1993) exploratory practice model, outlined in Chapter 1, the research group first identified a 'puzzle area'. Throughout their secondary school careers, pupils are expected to understand and produce a range of written discourse types. Despite being exposed to numerous example texts, pupils continue to show a number of weaknesses in their writing which could be attributed to an insecure grasp of features characteristic of specific discourse types. These features are rarely examined explicitly in the classroom, curriculum demands typically confining extended writing tasks to homework, thereby reducing opportunities for direct teacher intervention in the writing process. After a series of collaborative planning sessions, representing Steps 2 and 3 of the model, the research group refined its initial broad puzzle area – *the effects of the analysis of the structural features of a particular discourse type on pupils' production of this discourse type* – into (Step 4) the more focussed research question: *what effects, if any, does the classroom analysis of some of the discoursal features of fairy tales (narrative discourse) have on pupils' production of fairy tales?*

The Implementation Phase

The Classroom Procedures

A sequence of six lessons, representing Step 5 of the model, was taught over three weeks by Julia, the language support teacher, with the mainstream teacher present throughout. The mainstream teacher held a position of responsibility in the English Department and was co-ordinator of the Year 7 Foundation Curriculum, in which classes are taught English, History and Geography by one core teacher. Implementing the research project with her present, therefore, had good potential for the dissemination of findings across subject areas.

The first lesson served to activate students' formal and content schemata (Carrell and Eisterhold, 1988: 79) of fairy tales through a group brainstorming activity and the provision of a sample fairy tale. This was intended to replicate the kind of input prior to pupil writing which is typical of secondary school classrooms, where a model text is provided and some of its features are discussed but no detailed examination of discourse features takes place. The pupils then wrote their own fairy tales, providing the first sample of written output.

Through a series of activities in the second, third and fourth lessons, Julia attempted to go a step further and explicitly highlight some of the features typical of the narrative genre. The activities were based on the modern fairy tale 'Prince Amilec' by Tanith Lee (1986), and focussed on certain macro-structural features of narrative, following Labov's model (summarised in McCarthy, 1991: 137-142) – its beginning (abstract and orientation), middle (complication) and end (resolution). Attention was also drawn to more micro-structural features, such as use of the past tense, dialogue, and time expressions used as cohesive devices. This three-lesson sequence was followed by two further lessons in which pupils wrote their own fairy tales based on the new input.

The Data Collection Instruments

Two types of data were collected (Step 6 of the model). Lesson 2 was to be the main focus for the collection of data on the pupils' oral output. The class were paired and grouped on a mixed ability basis, pupils' personalities also being taken into account in order to create an environment maximally conducive to co-operative work and therefore language acquisition. A colleague from the LEAP team acted as observer for this lesson, filling in an observation schedule to record all pupils' use of the past tense when each group was asked to reproduce part of the narrative orally.

The idea for, and design of, the observation schedule emerged during the piloting of the project materials. Three of the activities in Lesson 2 focused on the three tasks that the princess sets Prince Amilec in order to win her hand. The structural parallelism of these three parts of the story, typical of many fairy tales, was exploited by extracting the outline of the narrative action from the original text and summarising it in the same sequence of thirteen simple past verb forms. The first activity required the pupils to listen to the teacher narrating the first of the princess's tasks and to number the verb forms in the order in which they heard them. The second activity asked them to listen to the princess's second task and arrange a set of pictures in the correct order. When asked to feed back on both these activities, individual pupils were able to use the correct sequence of verb forms, written on the board, as support for retelling each part of the story. In the third activity, the pupils prepared and presented a group oral narration of the princess's third task (all members of the group being required to make a contribution), working from a set of pictures similar to those in the second activity. The thirteen verb forms remained on the board for support if they needed it, but the pupils were otherwise free to create their own spontaneous response.

While listening to the group oral presentations during the pilot, it was possible to make only on-the-spot judgements about the language the pupils were actually producing. It was therefore decided to design an observation schedule on which it could be recorded a) whether or not pupils used the past tense forms provided; b) whether they used any other past tense verb forms; and c) whether they used any other tense in their presentations, notably the present. The schedule was designed to be as user-friendly as possible, with a first column listing the thirteen verb forms, a second column for the observer to tick which of the forms was used, and a third column to note the use of any other forms, past or present. The observation schedule thus employed a category rather than a sign system, allowing the observer to document a behaviour each time it occurred, and focused on low, rather than high, inference categories, requiring the minimum of interpretation on the part of the observer (Nunan, 1992: 97).

Allwright and Bailey (1991: 3-4) describe two ways of getting a record of what happens in a classroom. The first is to create a data base by direct observation, as outlined above. The second is:

> ...simply to ask, to give people an opportunity to report for themselves what has happened to them and what they think about it ...Although we must not assume that such ... questions are always answered truthfully, or even carefully, we can try asking people to tell us what happened to them in class, and treat their replies as our basic data, or at the very least as data to consider alongside whatever we have been able to observe directly.

In addition to the observation schedule, therefore, it was decided to elicit views on the narrative lessons from both the mainstream teacher and the pupils.

In the week following the lesson sequence, six target pupils (five bilingual pupils representing a range of oracy and literacy levels, and one native English speaker) were interviewed in pairs by the observer colleague, with Julia present. Julia also interviewed the mainstream teacher. All interviews were audio tape recorded. The questions for both the pupils and the mainstream teacher focused on a) the extent to which the pupils enjoyed the lessons; b) their understanding of the activities and their perception of the reasoning behind them; c) what they felt they had learnt about the discourse structure of fairy tales; and d) the difference they perceived between their pre-input and post-input written work. Although the interviewers had a list of pre-determined questions, they were intended to act as prompts rather than be strictly adhered to, allowing the interviewer flexibility to respond appropriately to the interviewees' comments (Nunan, 1992: 149).

A number of other considerations guided the conduct of the interviews. First, the interviews took place as soon as possible after the lesson sequence. Second, the interviews were not requested until after the lessons had been taught. Third, the pupils were unfamiliar with being asked what they thought about particular lessons, so they were interviewed in pairs to minimise the possibility of their feeling inhibited or threatened. They were also interviewed in the familiar environment of their classroom, rather than the more intimidating atmosphere of, say, the staffroom.

The Analysis and Evaluation Phase
Data Analysis and Findings
The class was divided into six groups for the oral narration exercise. Analysis of the observation schedules shows that one group (Group 3) used all thirteen of the targeted verb forms, three groups used twelve (Groups 1, 4 and 6) and two groups (Groups 2 and 5) used ten. Further analysis revealed that the pupils added extra forms where necessary, varied the order in which they used the provided forms (for example, reversing the order of *gave* and *handed*), and used synonyms (for example, *turned into* for *changed into*). Deviation from use of the past tense was observed in both monolingual and bilingual pupils, although, interestingly, only monolingual pupils used the present tense with forms which had been provided: for example, 'the prince *hands* the pearl necklace back' (Alan in Group 3). Problems were created for some of the bilingual pupils by the need to create language for the picture which showed the princess breaking her necklace. Two groups used *threw* or *dropped* correctly, a third group omitted to say anything, while the other three groups had to improvise (Metab and Sobia used **throw*, while Ikhlaq used **throwed*).

The interviews provided some revealing insights. Lessons 1 and 2 had a particular focus on listening skills, and three pupils said they enjoyed listening to the stories. The mainstream teacher also stated that she felt the class particularly enjoyed the listening activities ...'very engaged in this task – all of them' and 'whole class very engaged in numbering task'. In the activity where pupils listened in order to sequence the past tense verb forms, the class were provided with a specific purpose for listening, and the mainstream teacher commented that this was a strategy she intended to incorporate into her own teaching, but she also noted that she found the activity quite difficult. The activity has since been adapted to allow the pupils to listen to the princess's first task twice.

The oral pair and group work was another feature of the lesson sequence which met with approval. The mainstream teacher felt that the mixed ability groupings had given everyone the chance to speak and to contribute. She also liked the hands-on aspect of the activities, where the pupils had cards and pictures to manipulate. When Pupil B was asked what she had particularly enjoyed about the lessons, she mentioned the group discussion activity: '...when we were in the groups, in fours, and we had to do some work on the pictures – what's going to happen next, we had to work out what's going to happen next from the pictures'. The benefits of group work were summed up by Pupil C: '...with the group people, Miss, everyone helps you in it, in the group...'.

Question 3 investigated the pupils' perceptions of the purpose behind the lessons. Pupils A and F both used the phrase 'looking at' with reference to a number of activities, suggesting an awareness of purpose. One reason for the activities mentioned by the pupils was to get ideas for their own stories. When asked why he thought he had to listen to a fairy tale, Pupil F replied: 'so we know like what kind of thing to put into your own fairy tale, like the person, everything...'. Of the four pupils who considered their second fairy tale better than their first, two referred to learning more as the reason for this improvement: '... because, Miss, I, before I didn't know nothing about it, and Miss then we worked on it and I knew more about it' (Pupil D).

In terms of what they thought they had learnt about the structure of fairy tales, five pupils mentioned the formulaic beginnings and endings: 'Once upon a time...' and '... lived happily ever after', features which were high-lighted in Lesson 1 and which they used in their pre-input writing. Features specifically dealt with in the subsequent lessons and mentioned by the pupils were: places, tasks, time expressions, characters. Pupil E in particular gave an almost complete analysis of fairy tale structure and its constituent parts.

When questioned about the differences between their first and second written outputs, we see the influence of using 'Prince Amilec' as a frame-work. Pupil C emphasises the need to include tasks: '... the last time we did it, Miss, there weren't any tasks and this time we had to put some tasks in and ... then we had to just write a fairy tale, but this one has to be some-thing with the tasks...'. The mainstream teacher felt that improvements in their writing were due to having a discourse framework and the structure of the activities: '... they've got the structure of the tasks and they've got the framework there, they know if they've written one task, they know they have to go on to the second one and then on to the third one, whereas without that you just got maybe a little middle'. She also felt that there was more dialogue in their second attempts, a possible result of including *said* and *told* as verb forms in the list on the board.

A further point which emerged from the comparison of the written outcomes was the value of discussion in the drafting process. When asked where she got all the information from about things to write, Pupil A's answer was: 'Listening to other people's fairy stories and then thinking about your own work, if they're very similar to yours then just share it with them, some of the ideas'. The mainstream teacher also regarded opportunities for pupils to talk to each other about their work as useful.

Evaluation

Implementing the project had a number of benefits for Julia. First, she developed knowledge about research methodology and improved her own skills as a researcher. The project provided her with a sharper focus on her own practice, what was going on in her classroom and what effects this may have had on individual learners. It turned her into 'an explorer' in the classroom not only *during* the research project but, more importantly perhaps, *subsequently* (Allwright and Bailey, 1991: 13). Not only is she more aware of possible issues to investigate, but she is now in a better position to narrow the focus of any research question and adopt appropriate data collection and analysis procedures. All of the above, together with her enthusiasm to carry out further research, is reflected in Nunan's comment that 'the development of skills in observing and documenting classroom action and interaction, particularly if these foster the adoption of a research orientation by teachers to their classrooms, provides a powerful impetus to professional self-renewal' (1992: 103).

Second, the data collection instruments proved useful tools for providing feedback on her teaching. She had previously lacked a systematic way of examining the effects of her language teaching strategies and techniques, so analysing the pupils' oral outcomes through the observation schedule allowed her to assess more objectively the success of one particular teaching approach. The flexibility with which the pupils used the framework eased her concern that the provision of such a structure might inhibit creativity and differentiation, and restrict the achievement of more able pupils. Although the involvement of others was not absolutely necessary (she could have done it herself), asking a colleague to complete the schedule proved to be a good way of sharing ideas about the focus and effects of a particular technique or activity. This particular schedule has subsequently been used by other teachers when the lesson sequence was taught to other classes. Conducting interviews also proved fruitful and revealed aspects of the lesson sequence noticed and valued by the pupils and the mainstream teacher. The interviews highlighted the benefits for both pupils and teacher of asking pupils to reflect on their own learning. The six pupils interviewed showed a relatively high level of awareness of what was going on in the classroom and of the purpose of the activities. The data provided more substantial insights than those elicited from the written self-assessment more typically used in secondary schools. Interviewing the class teacher was a useful way of encouraging her to evaluate and reflect on an unfamiliar approach to the treatment of texts in the English lesson.

Third, the research project generally benefited both the target group of pupils and the class as a whole. The activities had a positive effect on their oral skills and awareness of some of the discourse features of narrative, and appeared also to develop pupils' analytic ability. The more explicit focus on and discussion of narrative structure appeared to contribute to the development of a metalanguage, enabling pupils and teachers to talk more fruitfully about the nature of language and text. Indeed, Julia felt that she was far more overt and specific about the discoursal features of text in her teaching than previously. The pupils also seemed to derive pleasure from participating in a research project, and enjoyed being interviewed. Being given an opportunity to voice their opinions perhaps increased their sense of their potential to be actively involved in the learning process.

For Mike, the project brought reassurance on a number of grounds. First, he had seen the input from his in-service course on discourse analysis – the 'theory' – find its way into the classroom – the 'practice' – in a very positive and constructive way. Julia's three lessons based on the 'Prince Amilec' story showed not only that a theoretical construct like that of Labov's could be used as a framework for materials design, but also that a conscious knowledge of that framework could aid pupils' understanding and production of appropriate language. Second, the project demonstrated that encouraging teachers to adopt a research-oriented culture could indeed improve their understanding of their day-to-day practice. They could use classroom and data collection procedures that grow out of normal practice and do not make excessive additional demands on their time. Through the observation by the language support colleague and the interview with the mainstream teacher, the project had also served to generate professional discussion about the content and methodology of language teaching, a debate that is too often highjacked by the necessary, but essentially mundane, concerns of school administration and pupil behaviour. This reinforced his conviction that peer observation and action research are two of the most successful modes of teacher development. Finally, the project confirmed his belief that teachers in schools and education lecturers in universities can find ways of working together that engage teachers more in activities that have traditionally been associated with lecturers (i.e. research) and keep lecturers more in touch with the traditional concern of teachers (i.e. the realities of the classroom), while recognising that their skills need to remain complementary if educational theory and practice are to make progress together.

Simpson and Tuson (1995: 3) sum up for both of us the overall justification for and impact of this research project.

At the end of your investigation you will still have not demonstrated beyond all doubt what exactly is going on, but if you have provided some systematically collected information on what may be going on, and have advanced your own thinking and the thinking of others, then your researches will have succeeded.

References

Allwright, D. (1993) Integrating 'research' and 'pedagogy': appropriate criteria and practical possibilities. In Edge, J. and K. Richards (Eds) *Teachers Develop Teachers Research: Papers on classroom research and teacher development.* Oxford: Heinemann.

Allwright, D. and Bailey, K.M. (1991) *Focus on the Language Classroom.* Cambridge: Cambridge University Press.

Carrell, P.L. and Eisterhold, J.C. (1988) Schema theory and ESL reading pedagogy. In Carrell, P.L., Devine J. and D.E.Eskey (Eds) *Interactive Approaches to Second Language Reading.* Cambridge: Cambridge University Press.

Lee, T. (1986) Prince Amilec. In Zipes, J. (Ed) *Don't Bet on the Prince.* New York: Methuen.

McCarthy, M. (1991) *Discourse Analysis for Language Teachers.* Cambridge: Cambridge University Press.

Nunan, D. (1992) *Research Methods in Language Learning.* Cambridge: Cambridge University Press.

Simpson, M. and Tuson, J. (1995) *Using Observations in Small-Scale Research: A Beginner's Guide.* Edinburgh: Scottish Council for Research in Education (SCRE Publication 130).

CHAPTER FIVE

In search of a role for email and the World Wide Web in improving the writing of bilingual learners

Diane Slaouti
University of Manchester

Stephen Pennells
King's High School, Manchester

Heather Weatherhead
Queen's High School, Rochdale

Introduction

This chapter explores a teaching and learning context that brought together language support teachers, a university teacher, second language learners and technology. The project involved collaboration between a lecturer from the University of Manchester (the author of this chapter) and two secondary school teachers. Both teachers provide language support to English as an Additional Language (EAL) learners in their respective schools: one in central Manchester (referred to as King's High School) and one in Rochdale (referred to as Queen's High School). The schools have large numbers of EAL learners: the one a mixture of Urdu/Punjabi, African-Caribbean and a variety of refugee learners, and the other mainly Urdu/Punjabi speakers. The final element was technology. Questions about its impact on the learners, on the learning environment and on classroom practice brought us together at a time when the UK government was encouraging the development of teachers' competence in the application of Information and Communications Technology (ICT) to their subject teaching[1].

Successful exploitation of ICT, however, is dependent on many variables. There is much to explore in the complex relationships between the characteristics of a specific technology: learning outcomes, learner types, and the way in which teachers situate these within a given methodology. The government-funded ImpacT study (Watson, 1993) concluded that IT does have a 'highly positive impact on children's achievements' but in *'certain circumstances'* (Johnson *et al*, 1994: 138). These circumstances include levels of access to IT, teacher variables such as teaching style and ability and levels of support within and outside school. Each school presents its own specific circumstances. The schools in our project were no exception. However, there were similarities in the need to support a large body of EAL learners. It was this particular variable that interested us. Could teachers find a meaningful role for ICT in the writing development of these particular learners in these particular learning contexts?

IT and the development of writing skills

The benefits of using word processing to develop writing skills are well documented. Claims are based on an acceptance of the links between the *process* of writing and the nature of the tool itself. Hayes and Flower (1980) presented one of the earliest models of the writing process and described the recursive process of *planning* (generating ideas, organising, setting goals), *translating* (putting into words, drafting) and *reviewing* (reading and editing). Their work revealed that these stages were variously influenced by the writing task, by knowledge of topic and audience, by stored writing plans and by the evolving text.

The word processor appears to come into its own in the *translating* and *reviewing* phases. Text can be produced, deleted, moved, and the fact that nothing is written in stone results in greater risk-taking (Cochran-Smith, 1991). Whether the ease with which text can be drafted and redrafted brings about improved writing is less well demonstrated, however. The relation between word processing and written output is not a simple one. Contextual factors play an important role. These, as Jessel (1997: 36) found, include learner attitude, teacher intervention, time, and the 'wider context within which writing occurs'. The wider context proved to be of particular interest in our own project.

The relationship between email and the writing process is less well documented. The use of email in school contexts is largely characterised by the 'keypal' idea – using email to put learners in contact with peers from other cultures, the motivation to communicate with the 'audience beyond the classroom' being the focus of attention (see Kroonenberg, 1995 for some examples in second language teaching contexts). Few studies explore email-generated writing itself. However, Kroonenberg, who reports on the relation between email activity and oral work, observes:

> Thoughts and arguments first composed in writing on email give students reflection time prior to engaging in oral work... the quality of the argument is enhanced and thinking is more creative than without this kind of preparation. (p.27)

This aspect of email use proved to be important in a pilot study of children using email, word processing and the World Wide Web carried out at King's High School during 1997.

The beginnings of the project

A small group of bilingual children was linked up with a group of teachers following a Masters course in ELT at the University of Manchester (Slaouti, 1997). These children, working with Stephen, exchanged messages with the teachers over a nine month period. These messages built up an autobiographical picture which was later assembled for 'web publication.' This pilot project allowed us to examine the email messages exchanged between partners and to discover the type of content they carried. The children appeared to focus on getting their ideas on to screen rather than on attending to accuracy. Although this seeming lack of attention to the language they used appeared frustrating at the time, this rehearsal ground provided support for a later and more public piece of writing for a web page, at which point there was a reason to edit for another type of readership. There seemed to be a possible role for email 'in the generation of ideas' stage of the writing process, a stage within which accuracy was less important but in which the knowledge of readers beyond the classroom resulted in a desire to put ideas in writing.

In an early diary entry, Stephen outlined his hopes for the link-up with Queen's High School planned for 1997-98.

I expected that greater integration with mainstream English would allow us to find out more about the strengths and weaknesses of email, word processing and www publishing used in symbiosis allowing for several stages of a writing process to be developed. The pupils would also have to actively consider differences of audience as the pupils taking part in the two schools had comparable but distinctly different linguistic and social profiles.

The unfolding of the project

Our aim was to explore further what we felt was a potential role for these technologies in the development of writing skills and to anchor these activities more firmly within the curriculum. We were particularly interested in the idea of email as a 'rehearsal tool' and the web as a publishing arena and to discover what sort of benefits these tools brought to the specific learners in these contexts. The children were to use email to establish rapport and then exchange ideas and texts on a topic that was part of their curriculum: the writing of folk tales. Given the cultures represented by the two groups, we felt that this could develop into a fruitful area of exchange. The stories would be developed using word processing and finally published on a shared web page for peer readership and perhaps beyond.

Stephen and Heather each selected a Year 7 class (11-12 year olds in their first year of secondary education). Although the children in the two schools came from very different communities, their need for additional language support was a unifying characteristic. The group in Queen's High School was a mixed ability class of twenty six pupils. Nine were from a white British background, two from a Bengali background and fifteen from a Pakistani background. Four of the children were targeted for language support. The King's School class consisted of nine African-Caribbean children, eight from a white British background, five Somali refugees and one child of mixed race. Five children in this group were targeted for language support.

Diary of events

April

- Teachers initiated pre-writing work on the genre of folk tales; the children spent time reading stories

- Link-ups between children in the two schools were set up

- 'Getting-to-know-you' messages were exchanged

- Teachers used writing frames to support children in generating ideas and writing introductions to their stories

- As some of the children were ready to share ideas, some exchange of drafts occurred.

At this point the project began to go awry in a way that none of us had predicted. King's experienced technical problems that became so frustrating that the very use of IT began to have a demotivating effect both on the children and on ourselves. This is a feeling echoed by so many teachers in contexts where technology provision is in either early or constant stages of development. We decided, therefore, to abandon the link at this point and the project continued at Queen's alone in the hope that King's children would at least be able to read stories from their peers at a later stage. I had to become the alternative audience.

May-June

- Queen's children continued to develop their stories and emailed their developing drafts to me

- I responded to their stories as a reader

- The children transferred their completed stories to their individual web pages, eventually brought together on the school web site

- Many of the children included their email address, inviting readers to respond.

These are the *events* of the project. It is what we take away from such events that constitutes professional learning. I shall now go on to describe how reflective practice in this project elicited that learning.

An action research approach

When we first met to talk through the project, we had certain hypotheses about the role of technology in the specific contexts of the two schools, but none of us could be sure of the outcomes. Although Stephen had been part of the previous year's project, neither he nor Heather knew exactly what was going to unfold from lesson to lesson. We were all familiar with the potential of word processing to develop writing skills but were not aware of projects which had attempted to bring the three technologies (email, word processing and the WWW) together in a structured framework such as this. Stephen and Heather had decided to research their own classrooms in order to develop their understanding.

Practitioner-based research models are frequently based upon the notion of establishing a question or a problem, planning and implementing an action, observing, reflecting and repeating. The problem or 'puzzle' (Allwright, 1993: 131) that a teacher would like to explore emerges from current practice. It is, therefore, anchored in the teacher's current knowledge base; it starts from observable events and seeks to move practice on from that point. However, the implementation of such a cycle in a classroom where technology is being explored may be different.

Technology for many teachers is a new and untested variable. There is, therefore, a certain leap into the unknown, which training and familiarity with technology may not adequately prepare teachers for. Being provided with the skills to use the computer and with ideas for classroom applications may not mean effective implementation. The starting point is, perhaps, a different one. Miller and Olsen (1996: 123) explore the relationship between technology and the evolution of a teacher's practice and suggest that it is the teacher's existing practice that influences the way in which the computer is used. The question is more likely to be: 'in the context in which I am teaching, with my learners and their needs, will technology contribute to my practice and how?'

The following model represents the framework and exemplification that emerged as the project developed (see figure 1).

The framework suggests a rather orderly approach, an impression that we must dispel. The narrative is a rather messy one. In the reality of the secondary school context, time to take notes, write legible and full diary

Stage	Application to current project
Identify and describe current practice	Teaching the writing of folk tales by using reading into writing frames. (We described practices during our first meeting as a group.)
Identify initial idea (formulated in terms of a statement)	Technological tools that involve 'writing' may contribute to developing the children's skills.
Analysis (possibly hypothetical as well as actual:	Reflection on the features of the tools identified and how they might 'fit into,' 'modify' or 'affect' current practice) • the nature of email as a tool for communication (the fact that it is in written mode but is associated with many of the features of spoken discourse) • the nature of word processors as a tool that can facilitate the drafting and editing of text • the nature of the Web as a potentially 'public display' arena for text, with scope to be read by audiences beyond the classroom.
Plan	Plan the full cycle of work and the moments at which the technological tools might be brought in as well as their possible impact on learning outcomes.
Implement and 'observe' Collect data	'Observation' included observing children on task, videoing some classes, collecting all email communications from pupil to pupil (saved to a central directory), collecting evidence of children's word processed writing at its different stages.
Notice and note	There were three stages to the 'noting' phase: immediate post-lesson exchanges often impacting on the next lesson; diary entries reflecting personal reactions as well as notable occurrences in the day's lesson; post-project discussions when we all met up to reflect on the sequence of events. Part of this post-project perspective was also the gathering of the children's observations on the sequence of activities. What we noted was either reflected upon immediately or noted in diaries kept by all participants.
Reflect, ask questions, attempt explanation	The following serves to exemplify some of the debate. The different email environments (one web-based, the other software-based) appeared to impact on the children's ability to remain on-task and subsequently on the learning outcome. Why was management of the same task in the two environments proving to be different? We attempted to describe the two email environments, discussed the nature of the 'literacy of the Web', its mix of visual and text-based messages, the fact that the children at King's were used to 'surfing' so were more tempted to move off-task, whereas the children at Queen's were not.
Revise	Revision meant both revision during the lifetime of the project and revision in subsequent cycles of similar curriculum work.

Figure 1: Practitioner-based research in technology: framework and exemplification.

entries, sit and discuss observations, and plan the next stage is scarce. However, the various perspectives afforded by the different 'noting' mechanisms gave us much food for thought.

Reflections about email

Types of system

Many of Stephen's diary entries and his post-project reflections focus on this area. This was obviously high on his agenda because of the difficulty his children experienced. However, beyond the technological difficulties, Stephen noted a specific phenomenon related to the email software being used. The children at King's were using a web-based emailing system called Mailexcite. This is a very different environment from the software-based email used at Queen's which is not far removed from a word processor. I was present at both schools during email sessions and the atmosphere in the classroom was very different, largely related to children's abilities to engage with their tools in order to accomplish their task. This led to much discussion between the three of us regarding contextual factors that might provide particular difficulties for our EAL learners.

The following extracts illustrate the concern. They also reflect the nature of the entries at different moments: the rushed and descriptive comments of Stephen's diary entries and the more reflective analyses from our post-project discussions.

Stephen: Friday May 8th

> Took Ashraf[2] and Ahmed to try to get them to complete their messages. Ahmed sent a fragment. Ashraf saved a draft. At lunchtime, spent some time with Hamda but she was not focused on the task or on mastering the system. Tanisha eager to get on. But didn't settle well to concentrating on her screen.

Diane: Friday May 8th

> Tanisha very enthusiastic today – had her first reply from Queen's. Didn't seem to last. At least not for the emailing. Watched her clicking on advertising buttons on the Mailexcite site – into some fashion area. Getting back to email area was complicated. (I had difficulty finding my way back, never mind Tanisha.)

Stephen reflected at more length on these early difficulties as he revisited his diary and discussed the project with Heather and myself.

> Most software packages are there simply as a tool. They don't invite you in like this. You've got advertising flashing at you. You have messages like 'Click here.' And what do the children do? They click here! You have a mixture of visual and textual messages too. Often the children were drawn towards the visual. Even when you're typing your message, the colours and flashing buttons are there inviting you in. Maybe that's a reflection of the way they respond to messages in society – a visual literacy? Maybe it's a particular distraction for the bilingual children – visual messages are more accessible than dealing with producing text? I think the only way to find out is to compare with another email package.

We spent a long time thinking through the nature of the tools we had used. Based on her own experiences, Heather recognised the potential for the environment to be both distracting *and* motivating.

> If you're setting the children a task there are too many distractions. And you've got to admit the distractions on the Net are really interesting. When I allow myself to float around, it's really good. Why shouldn't the children? The problem is maybe there's a time for floating and when we need to scaffold their writing then we need to think carefully about choosing a 'no-nonsense' tool that facilitates and doesn't add more for them to think about.

Length and accuracy

The children's messages varied in length and were usually not very accurate (a feature we had noted in our pilot study in the previous year). However, a significant difference was that those from the Queen's children were longer and had a greater range of content. The difference may have resulted from the pre-task work, suggesting that personal email was no different from other writing tasks in terms of the support it required. The children at King's were asked to write to their partners to introduce themselves. The children at Queen's were provided with a writing frame to help them generate something about themselves. The frame is reflected in the first message below. The reply to Nassrin is revealing in that it is one of several messages[3] in which children confess to not knowing what to write.

Subject: Re: hello

Date: Thu, 07 May 1998 04:45:36 –0700

>Hello my name is nassrin I am 12 year old and I go to queens high school my school is really >nice but I wish it was near my house Rochdale is a big twon it has a lot good houses also

>Rochdale is a nice town in my famliy there are four girls one boy. I lik reading and I lik music. We >have been reading fairy stories at school. We are doing our stories. I will send you mine.

Hello nassrin, my name is called Tanesha I am 11 years old.I go to King's High School and it's near my house too I don't have to far. My hobbys are swimming,music,singing an lots of other things I like. It was nice writing to you I don't know what to do or say so ill just say by see you later nice talking!

Reflections about technology in relation to the writing process

As the Queen's children pressed on with developing their stories using the word processor and finally transferring them to their web pages, our diary entries reflect more on these aspects.

Heather: Wednesday May 20th

> Children transferred introductions to word processor. Very slow process. Some produced very little by the end! They were being so deliberate about everything they typed. A lot of deleting and retyping going on. Even when they moved on to composing the next section together.

Diane: Wednesday May 20th

> Heather commented at the end of the lesson – next time she'd do some pre-tasks on the word processor. The children are desperately focused on getting each word right before they go onto the next. They need to understand what the word processor can do and how it relates to their writing.

These observations contrast with the following comment offered by one of the children.

> Word processing our stories was the best bit. It made us learn quicker. We should have wrote all the story out on the computer straight away because it was a waist of time when we did it on paper.

The children generally perceived the word processor to be a useful tool but some confessed to not having enjoyed using it, including a child who lost his text three times. Clearly the tool itself can be a source of frustration. Heather and Stephen realised that the children's developing ICT skills were a key factor. Certainly, in Queen's, the ICT co-ordinator had worked alongside the children ensuring that ICT skills were largely in place. At King's, Stephen had had to do much of the groundwork himself. This aspect of institutional collaboration was an important factor for all.

We had greater expectations of word processing being used to produce a polished text than we actually observed. Having used the word processor to generate their texts, the children were reluctant to return and re-edit them. Because a document printed out from the word processor looks good, the idea of working at a deeper level was hard for many.

Publication on their Web page provided a further stage of encouragement but, although some further editing took place, the children were far more taken with the physical appearance of their pages than the accuracy of the content. Heather and I both commented on the gasps of admiration that travelled around the computer room as child after child changed the background colour of their page. Similar excitement was heard as they saw their photographs emerge on the screen for the first time. Once this had been achieved, as far as they were concerned, their work was complete. They were very proud of their achievements.

> I learnt how to make a web page. That was brilliant putting my story on it. We can look at it on our computer at home.
>
> I thought the best bit was when I put my background colour in.
>
> I got a bit muddled up when I did my web page but it was okay in the end. I thought my story looked good. I put my email address at the end.

The accuracy issue provided us with a dilemma which we failed to resolve. We had expected greater development but we also recognised the achievements of many children who had produced far more extended texts than usual. Heather took up this point in discussion:

> When I showed the staff the web pages produced by 7N at an INSETT day, the reaction was 'Ooh. The kids produced that?' I was a bit worried about some of the accuracy, wondering what they would say but they were impressed. I think inaccurate text on a web page is a bit of a problem but when I thought about our aims, this was for a school link-up and I felt the accuracy was less important. It was more about motivation to write for the children, knowing someone else would read their stories. Having said that though, next time I would do more group editing before the web production stage, get the more able children to help. There was a lot of collaboration happening around the computers throughout the lessons, I think I could have made more of that.

Heather clearly recognised the motivational aspect of technology, as reflected in many of the children's observations. She went further. Her notes mention the fact that the pupils were nervous at the prospect of 'making a web page', as indeed she was at first, and they needed plenty of confidence boosting.

> The children look at it first and think, I can't do this, then start to do it and realise they can – and they're producing something that lots of people are going to see – it's a big boost to their self-esteem.

In contrast, Stephen commented on the dangers of raising children's expectations and then running the risk of letting them down if the technology failed to live up to those expectations.

> A major factor to think about is the potentially demoralising effect non-reply has upon writers. The vision of virtually instant global communication acts as salt in the wound of the frustrated audience. A project such as we

ran was at the mercy of students being able to respond, ie in school, with the system working, with access to the machinery of sufficient frequency and duration and with time to digest a message, formulate and send a reply. For EAL learners time is even more of an issue. In our project pupils at King's expressed frustrations at hiatuses and these began to have an impact on the motivation felt in the early days.

Final reflections

Our observations, notes and reflections on this project raise as many questions as answers. But that was what we aimed to do – to be in a position to have questions to ask. Sometimes these are not formulated with the boldness of a direct question, such as: 'why are the children finding it so difficult to stay on task when we know they want to email their partners?' but more tentatively: 'I wonder why they won't go back and work on their texts again?'. Such questions are followed by the beginnings of proposals such as 'Next time we need to...'

So what did we all learn from this? We all gained insights into how technology can and cannot work within the curriculum. We saw the excitement that the prospect of using email as a 'sharing tool' can engender; the sense of achievement that successfully producing extended, good-looking text for a public domain can bring to learners who struggle with writing. We saw evidence of the impact of contextual factors on outcomes: the demotivating power of an unstable technological system; the nature of the different tools that children have available to them and the way in which they require the user to engage with them; the all-important role of the teacher and their understanding of learner needs. We finally learnt that we could challenge assumptions about technology in relation to the school curriculum, that a collaborative project such as this can further thinking not only about how technology might play a role in the writing curriculum but also how teachers might make this 'technology thing' work for them. There is, however, further exploration and thinking ahead.

Acknowledgements

We would like to acknowledge the support of the two schools and specifically Hilary Williams, ICT Co-ordinator at Queen's High School, who was a key contributor to the outcomes of this project.

References

Allwright, D. (1993) Integrating 'research' and 'pedagogy': appropriate criteria and practical possibilities. In Edge, J. and Richards, K. (Eds) *Teachers Develop Teachers Research: Papers on classroom research and teacher development.* Oxford: Heinemann.

Cochran-Smith, M. (1991) Word processing and writing in the elementary classroom: a critical review of related literature. *Review of Educational Research* 61/1: 107-153.

Department for Education and Employment (1998) *National Grid for Learning Challenge: Open for Learning: Open for Business.* DfEE Publications on-line. www.dfee.gov.uk/grid/challenge/index.htm

Hayes, J. R. and Flower, L. S. (1980) Identifying the organisation of writing processes. In Gregg, L. W. and Steinberg, E.R. (Eds) *Cognitive Processes in Writing.* Hillsdale NJ: Erlbaum Associates pp 3-30.

Jessel, J. (1997) Writing words and building thoughts. In Somekh, B. and Davis, N. (Eds) *Using Information Technology Effectively in Teaching and Learning.* London: Routledge.

Johnson, D. C., Cox, M. J. and D. M. Watson (1994) Evaluating the impact of IT on pupils' achievements. *Journal of Computer Assisted Learning* 10/3: 138-156.

Kroonenberg, N. (1995) Developing communicative and thinking skills via e-mail. *TESOL Journal* 4/2: 24 – 27.

Miller, L. and Olson, J. (1994) Putting the computer in its place: a study of teaching with technology. *Journal of Curriculum Studies* 26/2: 121-141.

Slaouti, D. (1997) Motivating learners to write: a role for email. *CALL Review* January pp 9-13.

Watson, D. M. (Ed, 1993) *The Impact Report: An evaluation of the impact of information technology on children's achievements in primary and secondary schools.* London: Department for Education and Kings College, London.

Notes

1. By 2002, teachers are expected to have engaged in a programme of needs assessment and training that will develop their abilities to use ICT. Funding has been provided for schools to embrace the introduction of ICT across the curriculum and for the development of training programmes and the establishment of networked links via the National Grid for Learning (DfEE, 1998).

2. All the children's names have been changed.

3. Email messages are presented as they were written.

CHAPTER SIX

Practice-based inquiry and in-service teacher education: a Namibian experience

Hertha Pomuti
The National Institute for Educational Development, Namibia

Lindsay Howard
University of Manchester

Introduction

In this chapter we[1] describe and explore parts of the experience of the National Institute for Educational Development (NIED), a directorate of the Namibian Ministry of Basic Education (NMBE), working in partnership with two British universities to produce modular distance education materials for two upgrading courses for unqualified and under-qualified Namibian teachers. The guiding principle of the materials was lifelong learning through participatory forms of inquiry. We would like to present this chapter as one of the many cycles of inquiry that we engaged in during our work together. At the macro level it is an inquiry into the insider-outsider relationship as an effective international partnership and at the micro level into the development of an appropriate assessment procedure to promote learning and transformation through inquiry.

Background

Namibia gained her independence in April 1990 and made education its top priority by legislating for free, basic education for all Namibian citizens. The education system that the country inherited was a legacy of Bantu education underpinned with political oppression by the white minority and based on authoritarian principles that not only represented a white world-view but also operated within a racially segregated framework. The whole system suffered from severe inequities that ranged from curriculum provisioning to physical infrastructure to opportunities for qualifications and in-service. All decisions regarding education were passed down through the hierarchical structure, which meant the non-white school context in 1990 was characterised by poor learner performance, high rates of failure, repetition and drop out, large scale under-age and over-age enrolment, low levels of efficiency and in general low motivation on the part of both teachers and learners.

Independence and its concomitant participatory liberation ideology brought the rhetoric of reform to every sphere. The education vision was encapsulated in the Ministry of Education and Culture's policy document: *Towards Education for All* (MEC, 1993):

> ...as we make the transition from educating elites to providing education for all our citizens, we are also making another shift – from teacher-centred education to learner-centred education. (p.10)

The educational mosaic had shifted; the major components were still identifiable but re-arranged to establish the holistic nature of the new vision, outlined in four major goals that clearly aimed to redress the injustices of the past:

Access	the end of educating an elite
Equity	overcoming educational disadvantage
Quality	to be a right for all
Democracy	provision of an education in democracy through democratic education

The new educational ideology challenged the past view of knowledge. Knowledge was no longer viewed as static, or as something that belongs to 'experts', that has to be packaged by experts, in textbooks written and published by experts, and delivered to passive learners in classrooms as 'truth'. Today knowledge is regarded as being socially constructed; all practitioners and all learners are encouraged to be active, to engage in critical thinking, to observe, and to explore possible responses in collaboration with others and thus to construct their own meanings and understandings. Each person involved in education is responsible for ensuring equity, quality and the provision of access through engagement with democratic processes.

The changes brought by independence in Namibia came at a time of great technological advancement in the world as a whole. Global competition for economic markets and mass communication spread a sense of the world as a global village in which individual national economies are increasingly focused on securing high levels of scientific and technological competence and in which the western mode of education is viewed as the access route. This means that in Namibia there are struggles, on the one hand between its colonial past and the globalisation process, and on the other between western educational values and Namibian/African community values. Namibian schools, for example, exist in an environment whose forms of life, work, economy, family and morals are quite different from those spread by the forces of transnational globalisation. Thus Namibian teachers have to operate at the interface of two cultures each of which is encoded in a different language: an African home language and English, the dominant language of the economic market place.

While most national education systems are conservative and resist change, Namibia has, at least officially, welcomed change. The education sphere has embraced the opportunity to connect with the wider world from which it had so long been isolated. It regards the development of a critical pedagogical perspective as crucial if Namibians are to shift the power base and actively participate in the agenda of their own lives.

The Basic Education Teacher Development INSET Programme

The situation at independence in 1990 was that 36% of the nation's 13,000 teachers had had no professional training. To realise the educational vision, the MEC embarked on several initiatives which led to the birth of the Basic Education Teacher Development in-service programme. Planning and needs analysis led in 1993 to the introduction of a 3-year pre-service teacher education qualification, the BET Diploma, and in the following year it was adopted as a one-year pilot for an in-service programme. This became the BETD INSET programme.

Between 1994 and 1996 further developments took place and today the BETD INSET is a 4-year general preparation for unqualified or partly qualified teachers in Basic Education. It aims to strike a balance between theory and practice in that professional studies are both a separate component throughout the programme and integrated in the different subject areas. The BETD INSET combines face-to-face and distance modes. The former provides support to INSET teachers through contact sessions held in regional centres three times a year.

The Namibian (insider) – UK (outsider) Partnership

As the result of a tendering process, Namibia invited two British universities, the University of Manchester (UM) and the University of East Anglia (UEA) to produce materials for the BETD INSET course.[2] The two universities were commissioned to produce modular distance mode materials for the Educational Theory and Practice (ETP) and Lower Primary Education (LPE) courses. UM took responsibility for assisting with the Special Educational Needs strand in ETP, the whole of the LPE course and for the final production of the distance materials. UEA was responsible for the overall production of the ETP course and for ensuring that all materials were developed through an action research approach.[3]

To guard against the British universities being regarded as the outside experts and the Namibians as the insider passive recipients, it was decided that the partnership would follow the same collaborative cycle of inquiry as the BETD INSET teachers. As the weight of the material production lay with the UK writers, it was envisaged that the Namibians would take full responsibility both for revision of the modules and the production of further modules informed by a Practice-Based Inquiry approach.

Planning Together

Discussions were held on how the written materials might develop teachers' capacity to:

* transform practices in schools in line with the new philosophy of education

* commit themselves to constructing better understandings of the type of social action that supports democratic education in schools and the wider community

- see the broad vision contained in the national goal statements and accept that the meanings made from value concepts (eg. quality) would differ from context to context.

We decided to adopt the Critical Inquiry approach which had been introduced in the BETD PRESET programme but would be referred to as Practice-Based Inquiry (PBI) in the BETD INSET programme, as we were working with practising teachers. PBI, like action research (Carr and Kemmis, 1986), would turn on the concept of a cycle of inquiry involving *planning – acting/observing – reflecting – evaluating* the changes or improvements effected by an action. What was important for us was that in-built, systematic reflection would lead to practitioners modifying the action throughout the inquiry in a **recursive** rather than linear way.

The modules would be activity based and the activities would involve teachers in:

- engaging in cycles of inquiry about their daily practice

- different kinds of collaboration and dialogue with others

- forming support groups at school and BETD INSET cluster support groups for regular dialogue around modular themes.

We argued that the knowledge teachers constructed through these activities would be valued as it would be grounded in the practical concerns of their own contexts. We hoped that if the emphasis was on practitioners reflecting about action taken and then sharing in dialogue with others, a social energy would be created which, in turn, would encourage groups to support one another in effecting change.

Dissemination of the reform philosophy through the PBI framework was considered to be the lynch pin of change and hinged on establishing and maintaining an *effective,* laterally-structured communications network between all the members of the partnership. To ensure a multiple perspective, feedback on draft materials was collected regularly from the UK writing team, from NIED personnel, BETD INSET administrators and BETD tutors and teachers. This was done both electronically and via face-to-face contact during visits to Namibia.

Quality assurance of the modular materials was structured as a three-way process. John Elliott (UEA) was responsible for academic quality, particularly in relation to consistency with the principles of PBI. Lindsay Howard (UM), who had had eight years experience of working with Namibian teachers, both pre- and post-independence, took responsibility for the quality of materials in terms of the Namibian context, including attention to language level. She then submitted the revised materials to Hertha Pomuti who, through reference groups in Namibia, co-ordinated the final quality assurance and gradually assumed more and more responsibility for the co-ordination of the total production.

How would transformation be effected and ownership shifted to the Namibians? We recognised that the initial plans posed several challenges.

1. PBI might be seen as social engineering in the form of a foreign imposition not this time of a body of declarative knowledge but of procedural knowledge. Was an approach that aimed to enable Namibians to control and change their life conditions in harmony with a Namibian or western world view? Would the 'outsiders' be accused of cultural imperialism?

2. The Namibians' only experience of distance learning was of study guides which contained 'incontestable' knowledge to be learned for examinations.

3. The majority of the BETD INSET teachers and tutors had no prior experience of any aspect of these materials (i.e. the reform philosophy, the PBI approach, active distance learning etc).

4. The partnership might slide into a real insider-outsider divide whereby the 'outsiders' were the British universities delivering packaged modules to the 'insiders' the Namibians.

Taking these issues as a base to critically inform and analyse our work at regular intervals, we collaborated to produce the following materials according to our different contractual responsibilities.

1. A 3-part Introductory Guide[4]

2. ETP and LPE Modules 1-12.[5]

3. An Assessment Scheme

    This will be elaborated below as an example of the partnership in action.

4. A Tutor's Guide

    This was written as a dialogue between an outsider (inquiring) and an insider (answering the questions) in the UK, at the Namibians' request, to assist with explanation of the basic concepts at the first contact session.

The Partnership in Action: Developing the Assessment Scheme

We (the present writers) chose to share the development of the assessment process because it was arguably the one aspect of the project that really challenged past views of knowledge and legitimacy. Our story also serves as an illustration of the way we operated the structures outlined above to collaborate at the insider/outsider interface through a PBI approach. Our story is in four phases. Each phase comprises a work period at the different home bases and a work period in Namibia.

Phase I

Planning the initial design (Home base period)

Although the partnership did not want assessment to wag the module tail it was agreed that a well-designed assessment scheme was important. Broadly, the assessment procedure needed to:

*   provide teachers with practical experience of PBI

*   encourage dialogue between different stakeholders and thus sustain support groups to continue the dialogue

*   provide feedback on teachers' progress which would help us to modify our writing

*   provide teachers with experience of continuous assessment from which they would derive their own practical theories.

The first assessment scheme was identical for both modules. It required teachers to follow the same cyclical process as PBI so that they would continually hone their skills of *observation, description, interpretation* and *evaluation* but with different content, so enriching and broadening their content knowledge. At the end of each module unit, there was a reflective assessment frame. Teachers described the actions they had taken in the unit, reviewed the feelings they had experienced, stated what they had learned, and then made a plan for the next steps they considered necessary in their particular situation. The end of unit assessment was inter-related with the end of module assessment in that teachers were required to reflect about each end-of-unit action plan and then answer a series of questions about the implementation of these plans.

The partnership wanted to use the evidence collected to assess how far BETD INSET teachers were

1. adopting the PBI approach in their classrooms to promote change

2. participating in decision-making in their classrooms

3. involved in the social construction of knowledge

4. engaged in democratic processes and how far they engaged others

5. shifting from traditional examination based assessment to continuous assessment in their classrooms

6. able to access continuous assessment principles given that the module was written in English

7. forming and using their cluster support groups to discuss or resolve any of these issues.

Working together in Namibia (1)

The draft outlines of the assessment proposals had been shared and refined through the established paper flow. Meetings were held with various stakeholders in the different regions to share reflections and evaluate the scheme for final drafting. It became clear that the following points had to be taken into account when re-drafting:

1. Although the writers were responsible for generating assessment tasks, the role of assessing the teachers' products was the responsibility of the tutors, and their decisions would be moderated at NIED by random sampling. This would restrict the opportunity for struc-

tured dialogue between tutors, teachers and administrators as well as opportunities for peer or self-assessment. Furthermore, both tutors and administrators were largely unfamiliar with both the concept of PBI and continuous assessment.

2. There were limited resources available to support systematic training for assessors. The length of their preparatory session had been reduced from four to two days. This would affect tutor confidence to assess in any new format.

3. Pressure was mounting for an examination-based BETD INSET assessment. This raised concern that the traditional academic practices of the past might return and this would distort the approach of learning through inquiry.

It was agreed that the UK writers would create a set of criteria for assessing practice-based inquiry assignments. The criteria would seek to stimulate the necessary discussion among tutors and assessors and then between tutors, INSET teachers and NIED staff. The four point scale, already in operation in the BETD pre-service course, was recommended for the sake of consistency.

Phase 2

Planning the criteria (Home base period)

A set of assessment criteria was generated in the UK through a PBI approach led by UEA and then shared through the materials flow with the Namibian team. Although both insiders and outsiders considered the language of the criteria difficult to access, time was a constraint and it was decided the assessment should be circulated with Modules 1-3 and feedback collected at the next Namibian work period.

Working together in Namibia (2)

Meetings were held at the same work sites as the first visit, but with many more stakeholders, to gather data concerning the draft Modules 1-3. Assessment was the most frequently raised topic and the comments have been categorised as follows:

- The assessment is repetitious

  There is too much assessment and it is always the same.

  It is so boring and I often do not do the end of unit ones.
  (BETD INSET teachers)

- Uncertainty around 'correctness'

  I do not know if I have put the right answer.

  My friend got a B and so did I but we had different answers. The tutor must have made a mistake!

  (BETD INSET teachers)

- Signposts of progress are missing

  Teacher A:　　　　　　I always get a 'C'.[6]

  Teacher B:　　　　　　*We all get Cs – all the time. I do not know why or where I am wrong.*

  Teachers A and C:　*We do not know what we must do to improve.*

  (3 teachers at Ondangwa West)

- Access to academic language of the criteria is difficult

  Even when I look in the dictionary I cannot follow the meaning.

  My tutor told me to read the criteria. I did that and I think I understand the English but I still cannot quite follow them.

  (BETD INSET teachers)

  The language is too tough for the teachers.

  We need a workshop to help us understand and use the criteria so we know what we have to do.

  (Tutors from Ongwediva and Rundu)

- Rationale is unclear

Where does it say that I must implement the end of unit action plan? Well I did not do that and so at the end of the module it was difficult to say how my action plans had been – I did not know what action plans it meant – but now you have explained...'

(BETD INSET teachers Ondangwa West)

Some of the teachers I work with show me the assessments finished but they have not done all the activities. When I asked them how they did the assessment they say they made it up.

(Tutors from Ongwediva and Rundu)

- The logistics are not manageable

These comments refer to the oral reports of the teachers about the changes they had made in school.

Most of us tutors, we have got 60 students and so it is impossible to listen to so many in two days.

I do not have so many INSET teachers but most of them are young ladies and they are shy to talk to me – an older male.

The teachers are very afraid as they do not know if what they have written is correct and so they do not want to talk.

(BETD INSET tutors)

Evaluating

On collectively evaluating the data we concluded that:

- Thinking about assessment was still tied to the past when information had been delivered in study guides from which the 'right answers' were selected to answer examination questions. The culture of dependency was still strong among the BETD INSET teachers who were interpreting the concepts with inappropriate frameworks from the past. We realised we had not generated enough dialogue to enable stakeholders to make shifts in their practice.

- The English words had not assisted the shift in understanding – some teachers were unaware that the assessments were inter-related, which meant they could not complete the end of module assessment until all the end of unit assessments had been carried out.

- The content seemed to have been overshadowed by the process and the rationale for the process was not clear.

- An oral report as part of the assessment task was not feasible at this time.

Phase 3

Planning a workshop (Home base period)

A workshop was planned for the tutors with the aim of discussing the principle of learner-centredness, whereby the participants would generate their own professional knowledge and understandings of learner-centred assessment.

Working together in Namibia (3)

Day 1: Tutors shared their experiences and then read a UK prepared paper to compare the author's understandings of learner-centred education with their own understandings. The purpose of the paper was to lead participants from definitions of learner-centred education, to understandings that they supported with contextual evidence, and to using that evidence for the development of criteria in terms of what was accepted as good Namibian practice.

Day 2: Tutors engaged in a cycle of inquiry that asked them to reflect-evaluate-plan-act. First they selected one of the modules and reflected on how they might construct an end of module task that would require the teachers to enrich and deepen their understandings of learner-centred education. An example of a possible end of module task was then shared and analysed in terms of the principle before groups of tutors constructed their own examples.

From the oral feedback at the end of the workshop, comments were categorised as follows:

- Expectations (tell me what to do) not met

  This contact session has been conducted through learner-centred methods and I enjoyed that and have learned much about it. But I did not have enough time to hear about how to assess the students.

  I did not come to design an assessment scheme or assessment task. I want to know what to tell the students — I mean how they must do their assessments.

- Awareness of being involved in a process of inquiry

  This has been good as I begin to understand the shift. I am going to share these examples with my students and we will discuss them as we did here.

  We need to know that we cannot be good at this straight away. It is a very different philosophy and it needs different work and it will take more time. Some do not want that but I think it is good as we can only learn by thinking more about what we are doing and why.

- Awareness of the need to be involved

  I understand we need criteria but these are too difficult — let's make them easier.

  I really feel I have learned how to develop myself and when I share this — if I can do it well — my students will be very happy.

Evaluating the feedback

The tutors had engaged with the activities even if they did not feel their particular needs were being met. However, we were concerned that the different purpose of the session (i.e. an activity-oriented workshop) had not been clearly communicated to or accepted by all participants and that this probably contributed to the view that not all the tutors' expectations had been met. The partnership engaged in vigorous discussion around all the questions posed at the outset and whether activity-based assessment was not a step too far, too soon. This led to renewed arguments for some sort of examination to focus tutors' and teachers' attention on the rationale underpinning the learner-centred assessment process. It was argued that the use of a familiar technique would encourage engagement with what had to be done in the modules and would also divert teachers away from pretending to complete the activities and from copying others' work.

Phase 4
Renewing the plan (Home base period)

Despite being aware that an examination might distort assessment through inquiry, we devised the end of module assessment task as an open-book examination. It is written at the contact session on completion of the module and still follows the PBI approach. The examination task is printed in each module so that the BETD INSET teacher is aware that completing the end of unit assessment is the preparation that needs to be done. This serves to make the link between the end of unit assessment and the end of module examination explicit. Teachers are asked to **describe** what **they** did in each end of unit assessment and to bring these descriptions, together with any evidence they have collected, to the contact sessions for the open-book end-of-module assessment.[7]

Conclusion and evaluation

It is not possible to evaluate the action further as the new assessment has not been implemented at the time of writing but what we can evaluate is how far we have come in the process. If we situate the year's activity within its total frame, we recognise the enormity of the task: to transform, through print distance materials, 1,500 teachers who were in 1990 thoroughly familiar with uni-lingual, uni-cultural transmission teaching assessed through formal examination.

All the action is for social change and the research is situated in the teachers' daily practices. The Namibian insiders are becoming increasingly involved in the inquiry process both at the level of their own practice and at the level of the whole design process for the BETD INSET distance programme. Their voices have increased in number and volume, the outsiders are listening, and action strategies are planned based upon collective wisdom. This process gradually produces more confident tutors and teachers who are ready to critically inquire and discuss what different actions mean in their contexts and how they might enrich current educational values. They are becoming socially active; they realise that by supporting each other much can be achieved not only in terms of concrete actions but also in terms of understandings.

Namibian practitioners tell us where we are one year on:

> • *We have really developed. We have really learned as we have groups that meet regularly and we talk about what to do. I hope these continue after we get our Diplomas. I think it will. We must do it.*
>
> (BETD INSET teachers)
>
> • *Do you remember I asked you at the first meeting who would Namibianise these modules and now I understand your answer: 'you will' – (laughing). We are, we really are doing it, aren't we?!*
>
> (BETD INSET tutors Ongwediva)

References

Carr, W. and Kemmis, S. (1986) *Becoming Critical: Knowing through Action Research.* Lewes: Falmer Press.

Ministry of Education and Culture (1993) *Towards Education for All: Development Brief for Education, Culture and Training.* Windhoek: Macmillan /SIDA.

Notes

1. Lindsay Howard is now Technical Adviser for Teacher Education, Department of Education, Eastern Cape, South Africa.

2. The contractor was the Teacher Education Reform Project (TERP), Umeå University, Sweden.

3. The two universities had been selected on the basis of their commitment to action research as the means to achieve the MEC's educational vision.

4. Part 1 is a description of the BETD INSET and the roles and responsibilities of all stake-holders and was written by NIED. Part 2 provides activities to focus practitioners' attention on ways they can become active distance learners through a PBI approach while Part 3 explores the philosophy and principles of the educational reform within a PBI approach. These two parts were written by the British universities.

5. Each module comprises an Activity Booklet and a Support Materials Booklet. The Activity Booklet provides teachers with opportunities to explore each modular theme

in their classrooms and in the wider community through systematic inquiry. The teachers are directed to the Support Materials at specific points in the Activity Booklet either to hone the skills needed for PBI or to provide alternative or richer perspectives on the modular theme. Teachers are required to interact with these materials and monitor the use of the concepts in their own contexts or alternatively challenge the appropriacy of the texts in their situations.

6.   A grade 'C' symbolised a Complete or 'pass' grade in the four grade system. Below 'C' was 'Incomplete'.

7.   The open-book assessment task requires teachers to:

- Describe what improvements/changes they wanted to make (here they will refer to the plans they wrote for the end of each unit assessment)

- Describe the evidence they collected. State how this evidence supported that such a change/improvement needed to be made

- Describe the different possible actions that were considered and support the choice of the action they took with evidence from the activities or from the support materials

- State which of the action plans that they wrote in the RESOLVING box at the end of each unit they have carried out or have tried to carry out

- Describe the methods they used to monitor the action and give the reasons why they chose them

- State the results and give reasons for them

- State what they want to do to further the inquiry within this module topic.

CHAPTER SEVEN

Writing to learn: a bottom-up approach to in-service teacher development

Kyung-Suk Chang
University of Manchester

Mike Beaumont
University of Manchester

Introduction

This chapter exemplifies one kind of collaboration that can occur during the process of doctoral research. The writers are the researcher (Kyung-Suk Chang), an English teacher from Korea, and the supervisor (Mike Beaumont). However, the research also involved the active participation of a number of practising English teachers and their pupils in Korean secondary schools.

Three Perspectives on Teacher Development

We begin by citing a series of quotations to outline the three different notions of teacher development which lay at the heart of this research project. The first relates to the role classroom teachers play in educational change, the second to the desirability of involving teachers in researching their own practice, and the third to the methods they use to do so.

The Management of Innovation

Changes can be proclaimed in official policy, or written authoritatively on paper. Change can look impressive when represented in the boxes and arrows of administrators' overheads, or enumerated as stages in evolutionary profiles of school growth. But changes of this kind are ... superficial. They do not strike at the heart of how children learn or how teachers teach. They achieve little more than trivial changes in practice. Neither do changes in buildings (like open-plan ones), textbooks, materials, technology (like computers), nor even student groupings (as in mixed ability groups) unless profound attention is paid to processes of teacher development that accompany these innovations. (Hargreaves, 1994: 10-11)

In many parts of the world, ELT is developing against a background of institutional and classroom constraints that inhibit change, creating a basic concern about the feasibility of individual teacher development within such contexts. In a state system, changes to the syllabus, to teaching materials and to methods are typically imposed by the educational authorities. As Hargreaves (1994) makes clear, this traditional top-down approach frequently fails to bring about changes in the attitudes of classroom teachers and therefore their practice. In consequence, there is an increasing demand for the active participation of classroom teachers in the change process. Consequently, attempts need to be made to identify the perceptions, problems and interests of teachers if a clear understanding is to be reached of the sorts of difficulties teachers face in their everyday teaching situations. Such an understanding should inform the content and organisation of INSET programmes and opportunities for teachers to play an active role in such courses should be increased. Most importantly, it is crucial to develop sensitive and supportive environments in which teachers can improve their professional lives by having the confidence to change.

Practitioner-based Research

... action research is justified on the grounds that it is a valuable professional development tool. It represents what I would call an 'inside-out' approach to professional development. It represents a departure from the 'outside-in' approach (i.e. one in which an outside 'expert' brings the 'good news' to the practitioner in the form of a one-off workshop or seminar). In contrast, the inside-out approach begins with the concerns and interests of practitioners, placing them at the centre of the inquiry process. (Nunan, 1993: 41)

Fundamental to the action research movement is the argument that teacher-initiated classroom research is an effective, some would argue the only, way to bridge the gap between theory and practice. The principle is that research by teachers should grow out of the problems and issues which confront them in their daily work and the outcomes of such research therefore feed directly back into the classroom. As Nunan (1989:15) and many others maintain, teachers' exploration of their own classrooms should lead them from practice to theory and back to practice again as a kind of on-going professional growth spiral. Similarly, Ramani (1987) shows the way teachers can move towards 'theory discovery' through investigating issues they are interested in, thus making theory relevant to their everyday teaching. In this process, and over time, action research may contribute to the overall research base, but in essence it is more concerned with teacher development than it is with the generation of hard data.

Research Methodology

> ... we see most value in investigations that combine objective and subjective elements, that quantify only what can be usefully quantified, and that utilise qualitative data collection and analysis procedures wherever they are appropriate. (Allwright and Bailey, 1991: 67)

> As a research genre, diary studies are part of a growing body of literature on classroom research ... They are examples of participant observation that fall within the 'anthropological approach' to classroom research ... in the hermeneutic (interpretative) tradition ... My concern here, however, is not so much with diary studies as a mode of research but rather as potential tools for teacher preparation. (Bailey, 1990: 215)

This project (fully reported in Chang, 1995) was organised in two phases, an initial quantitative phase complementing a subsequent qualitative stage, consistent with the view of Allwright and Bailey quoted above. The quantitative phase used a questionnaire to investigate the attitudes of teachers and learners of English in Korean secondary schools to current approaches to the teaching of writing. The second phase adopted a qualitative approach, presenting teachers with significant findings from the questionnaire data and encouraging a small group of volunteer teachers to engage in small scale action research projects. In the first phase, the researcher adopted a traditional role in the design, conduct, analysis and reporting of the research. In the second phase, she essentially acted in a facilitating role, helping and supporting the teachers in their own research projects, using qualitative research tools to assist them in their professional development, most notably the keeping of teaching diaries.

The Context of the Study

The study was carried out in a context typical of many education systems (in the developed as well as the developing world) and which can be characterised by reference to four clusters of issues: those relating to the curriculum, to teaching methodology, to classroom conditions, and to teacher training. Together, they may be said to result in the kind of top-down, centralised and prescriptive system we outlined earlier in this chapter.

In the Korean secondary education system, English is not only a compulsory National Curriculum subject, but the list of textbooks which teachers may use is also prescribed by the Ministry of Education. Further-more, at school level, the specific textbook to be followed at a particular level is typically chosen by a committee of senior staff. A consequence is that the ordinary, practising classroom teacher has little or no choice over the materials to be used. An additional complication is the gap between the espoused 'communicative' principles of the National Curriculum and the more traditional characteristics of the textbooks themselves, creating a teaching culture that sticks with the familiar, rather than experimenting with the new. This conservatism is compounded by a highly competitive, exam-oriented system in which teachers, understandably, concentrate on training students to pass the exam rather than helping them to acquire real-world language skills.

The combined effect of a system which is exam-driven and which inhibits innovation and change is a teaching methodology that might comfortably be described as 'traditional'. A grammar-translation approach is pre-valent, resulting in an emphasis on the detailed explanation of gram-matical rules and of the meanings of unknown words. In terms of the receptive skills, there is a heavy emphasis on reading comprehension and a consequent paucity of time devoted to listening skills. Productively, accuracy is prized at the expense of fluency, and the writing skill, as well being preferred to the development of oral skills, is essentially used as a device for the pupils to practise, and demonstrate knowledge of, gram-matical rules.

Classroom conditions inhibit the development of communicative skills. Numbers are large – class sizes of 51-60 pupils are commonplace – and classes are mixed ability. Marking loads are therefore excessive, further curtailing the time and energy teachers have available for rethinking their practice. Overall, therefore, the situation encourages a teacher-centred methodology, where the scope for pupil involvement through more learner-centred activities is extremely limited.

Finally, teacher education systems model and reinforce many of the characteristics we have described. Initial training is heavily theoretical and exam-oriented, teaching practice being limited to the first semester of the final year of training. Trainee teachers are caught in a familiar vicious circle of language (in)competence. The traditional teaching in the school system produces students who are good at exams but who lack the communicative skills necessary to operate routinely in English. Teaching in higher education essentially gives them more of the same, feeding back into the secondary system teachers who lack both the language competence and the methodological repertoire to introduce more communicative techniques into the curriculum. In-service provision is similarly focused, requiring teachers to sit a formal exam after three years of training in order to progress up the professional ladder; whatever Masters courses exist are theoretically, rather than professionally, oriented.

The Study

For reasons partly outlined above, the study summarised here chose to focus on the teaching of writing, although its complementary aim was to judge the feasibility of teacher development through action research. To begin with, we recognised that the teaching of writing in Korean classrooms was characterised by what has been termed a 'product-oriented' approach, that is, an (over)emphasis on the text produced by the pupil, and therefore on feedback that is concerned essentially with the formal accuracy of the text. We were concerned, therefore, to investigate to what extent this was the case and what the attitudes of teachers and pupils were to this approach. Equally, we wanted to know to what extent teachers were experimenting with a more 'process-oriented' approach, that is, an approach which recognises the immense complexity of the writing process and the need for pupils to be engaged in dialogue about their writing and therefore be provided with feedback during the course of writing, the implication being, of course, that in the end this approach produces better writers (for detailed discussion of the product-process distinction, see, amongst many others, White and Arndt, 1991). However, we were not content with simply finding out what was happening. We wanted to move the project into a second phase, in which we intended to present the teachers with the results of the survey, and invite them to take part in a teacher development project, whereby they would set up an innovative practice in their teaching of writing, and chart its progress through a diary study. The following two sections describe in greater detail the conduct of these phases.

Phase 1: Identifying Problems

In an effort to gain insights into both pupils' and teachers' attitudes towards writing in the secondary English lesson, parallel questionnaires were designed to see how far the two parties agreed about various key issues. The questionnaire was divided into three sections matching the following general research questions:

- What do pupils and teachers think about the current product-oriented approach to the teaching of writing?

- What do pupils and teachers think about the conventional way in which feedback on writing tasks is provided?

- To what extent are aspects of a process-oriented approach to writing already being applied in the Korean secondary classroom?

Two hundred and one pupils and thirty two teachers of English from six secondary schools in Korea completed the questionnaires. Statistical analysis of the resulting data produced a number of interesting findings, the most significant of which were:

- Despite exam pressures, the pupils' attitudes to the current product-oriented approach to the teaching of writing were far more negative than those of the teachers, suggesting that they were more open to the idea of change than their teachers.

- There was a marked discrepancy between the perceptions of pupils and teachers about the amount of feedback provided on students' written work – teachers believed they supplied far more feedback than pupils thought they received.

- Despite various contextual factors that were inimical to change, both pupils and teachers agreed that certain aspects of a process-oriented approach to writing were of value. These included: carrying out writing tasks in pairs or groups; provision by the teacher of individual help to pupils during the writing process; and the motivational value of the provision by the teacher of positive comments on the pupils' written products, rather than the more traditional error-focused feedback.

The researcher then wrote to the teachers who had taken part in the survey, detailing the main findings, and inviting them to a meeting to discuss the implications. Ten of the thirty two original respondents attended the meeting, and three volunteered to take part in a follow-up teacher development project.

Phase 2: The Teacher Development Project
The teacher development project set out to help the three teachers become more aware of new ways of teaching EFL writing, systematically record their new teaching experiences, and share their reflections at regular meetings. The project group therefore met fortnightly to review progress, identify and discuss problems, exchange information, reflect on recent teaching experiences, and collaborate on ways forward. Each teacher undertook to investigate a particular dimension of the process writing approach. Their individual aims were:

- to improve pupils' writing through a process of drafting and redrafting

- to increase pupils' motivation to write through collaborative group work and

- to create a more co-operative atmosphere through peer correction.

From the researcher's point of view, the second phase of the study aimed to examine the process of the teachers' attitude change and individual professional development. The main research questions were:

- How does awareness-raising through critical reflection have an impact on instructional decision-making in the classroom?

- Does teachers' active participation in their own research projects result in increased commitment to change in teaching?

- Is ownership of change essential to the changing of teachers' attitudes and classroom practice?

- What benefits do teachers' own investigations of teaching writing bring to pupils as well as teachers themselves?

As attitude change and professional development are internal and personal, the research questions were investigated primarily through a first-person diary kept by the teachers. By agreement, these diaries were handed to the researcher for analysis. However, to obtain a more complete picture, and to include the perspectives of the researcher and the pupils as well as those of the three teachers, data from four other data sources were also used. These were: field notes written by the researcher (particularly in the meetings with the teachers), structured interviews with pupils, lesson plans, and classroom observations by the researcher.

The diary entries were carefully scrutinised and significant issues were systematically grouped, following a procedure adopted by Murphy-O'Dwyer (1985). Key criteria for selecting issues were recurrence and salience. That is, some issues were identified because of the frequency with which they were mentioned; others were selected because they were of particular significance and relevance to the research questions.

The Findings

This section gives a predominant voice, through the data collected, to the teachers and their pupils. Four main themes were identified.

Attitudes towards research/theory

Data from the diaries confirmed the view many teachers hold about their relationship with research and theory. First, they perceived a gap between theory and practice:

> Researchers try to discover more information about the composing process and studies appear to be flourishing as more and more appear in academe. However, it is a very new area for those of us who are involved in classroom teaching.

Second, they noted the inaccessibility of many research findings:

> In most cases, the results of research carried out in the school were not available so teachers and students forgot about it. We hardly get any feedback from the researcher so we feel like guinea pigs.

Third, they commented on the domination of top down decision-making:

> Education is very much governed by bureaucrats who make decisions for teachers in the classroom. The authorities have little respect for teaching. University researcher-experts are looked to as the sole source of knowledge. Teachers have no hope of ever gaining the power to change things.

Areas of change and growth

Three themes emerged in the teachers' entries on this issue. First, the action research project had helped them to develop a 'spirit of enquiry':

> At the local meeting, I said that the classroom research forced me to reconsider my work, and I think that was beneficial to my teaching. Research makes me think. While I write down my reflections, my thoughts get clearer. It is important to think about my job and what I am trying to achieve.

Second, the diary-keeping had served to refine their awareness of their own writing processes:

> I made persistent errors in writing. It makes me lose my temper just as I did over persistent errors in the students' writing. It seems to me that all the knowledge of grammar is not working properly in my case any better than it does in students' cases.

Third, they recognised that the project had begun to give them ownership of the process of change:

> I played the key role in setting up my own strategies through the classroom investigation and through reflective teaching. I found my own part in teaching in my own context, my working situation.

The importance of collaboration

The teachers commented on two ways in which a spirit of collaboration had been fostered. First, between the teachers and the researcher:

> The project I am involved in is characterised as collaborative and non-directive. A relationship of mutual trust and support has been established between the parties. We are not told 'This is the way you should do it'.

Second, they recognised the benefits of meeting each other and discussing their classroom experiences:

> It is becoming clear that there is need for more dialogue in the area of English language teaching. I have noted that effective development can take place through a sharing of experience between teachers within schools or from different schools.

Benefits to students

The interviews with pupils confirmed that the innovations which the three teachers had instigated had met with a positive response. First, the pupils appreciated the process of peer reviewing:

> When I read my writing, I couldn't see what was missing. Then my partner read it through and gave me a lot of useful advice about my writing, particularly in terms of content. She gave me her opinions.

Second, they felt that, through the process writing approach, they had achieved a greater control over their use of written English:

> I began to develop some understanding of what I can do in writing. This helped me feel more secure in using English.

Third, their attitudes to writing in the classroom had become more positive:

> I used to hate composition...My teacher got angry about so many grammatical mistakes. It made me agonise over grammatical perfection and hate writing. Now, I am experiencing a kind of achievement because my teacher is trying a different method, which is supportive. I am relaxed and write without anxiety over writing. I am gaining enthusiasm for writing.

Some caveats

We would not wish to create the impression that the teacher development project was an unqualified success. The data also threw up a number of disturbing observations. First, there was the authoritarian attitude of one deputy head teacher: 'The class was getting noisy as the groups worked with their drafts ... I didn't realise that the deputy head teacher had entered the classroom ... He started to discipline the class in front of me. It totally undermined my authority'. Second, there was the constant threat of being judged on results: '... the quality of learning was equated with the examination results ... I am afraid of being far from the norms of the group in the school ... of losing the headmaster's trust'. Third, there was the fear of an inexperienced teacher being involved in new practices: '... as a novice teacher, I am afraid of being isolated by the other seniors'. Fourth, one teacher worried about career progression: '... soon there is a term inspection by an outsider from the local education authority. If I try group work in the writing class, the class will be very noisy. If the noisy class is inspected by the authority, there will be possible loss of reputation and promotion prospects'. Finally, there was awareness that the culture of dialogue and co-operation flew in the face of local norms: '... it is very likely to be alien to teachers. Here, emphasis is given to acceptable public behaviour rather than openness in their relations with others.'

Conclusion

Despite these qualifications, the project was significant for us in at least three respects: first, it reassured us that teachers can introduce innovations even in contexts where a top-down approach to educational change is dominant; second, it reaffirmed our conviction that teacher development thrives when teachers are involved in the process of researching their own practice; and third, it demonstrated that quantitative and qualitative methods can be effectively combined in the investigation of complex educational issues.

Acknowledgements

We owe most to the three teachers without whose hard work and co-operation this study would have been impossible. One is currently involved in a co-operative development project with native speaking teachers in his school; one is following a part-time MA course; the third is pursuing her studies in the United States.

References

Allwright, D. and Bailey, K.M. (1991) *Focus on the Language Classroom: An introduction to classroom research for language teachers*. Cambridge: Cambridge University Press.

Bailey, K.M. (1990) The use of diary studies in teacher education programs. In Richards, J.C. and Nunan, D. (Eds) *Second Language Teacher Education*. Cambridge: Cambridge University Press pp 215-226.

Chang, Kyung-Suk (1995) *A Case Study of Teacher Development with Special Reference to Teaching EFL Writing in Korean Secondary Schools*. Doctoral Thesis, School of Education, University of Manchester.

Hargreaves, A. (1994) *Changing Teachers, Changing Times*. London: Cassell.

Murphy-O'Dwyer, L.M. (1985) Diary studies as a method for evaluating teacher training. In Alderson, C. (Ed) *Lancaster Practical Papers in English Language Education* Vol. 6: Evaluation. Oxford: Pergamon pp 97-128.

Nunan, D. (1989) *Understanding Language Classrooms: A guide for teacher-initiated research*. London: Prentice Hall.

Nunan, D. (1993) Action research in language education. In Edge, J. and Richards, K. (Eds) *Teachers Develop Teachers Research: Papers on classroom research and teacher development*. Oxford: Heinemann pp 39-50.

Ramani, E. (1987) Theorising from the classroom. *English Language Teaching Journal* 41/1: 3-11.

White, R.V. and Arndt, V. (1991) *Process Writing*. London: Longman.

CHAPTER EIGHT

Disseminating a Cultural Studies syllabus for foreign language teaching in Bulgaria: collaborative classroom research

Leah Davcheva
The British Council, Sofia

Richard Fay
University of Manchester

Introduction

On an autumn afternoon in 1998, we drove from the Bulgarian capital, Sofia, to the town of Ruse to participate in a new chapter of the large-scale cultural studies project that had begun five years earlier. Reliving the story of this project, the five-hour journey to Ruse passed quickly and we were eager to begin the seminar. This was a two-day event in which foreign language (FL) teachers would be introduced to the *Branching Out* syllabus (British Council, 1998). The syllabus had been produced by Bulgarian FL teachers, a bottom-up endeavour now formally recognised by the Ministry of Education and Science. It presents an approach to teaching about other cultures in the FL classroom which, although in keeping with recent thinking about cultural studies (eg. Byram, 1997), contrasts with the traditional transmissive and knowledge-based approach dominant in Bulgarian schools.[1]

The Ruse seminar would be the first of twenty two in coming months, a programme of teacher development across the nation involving hundreds of FL teachers. Each seminar in the series would initiate small-scale classroom research projects in which teachers would experiment with the cultural studies innovations. Six months later, they would reconvene to share their perceptions of the new approach. As we tell this story (combining insider and outsider perspectives),[2] we set out the principles and procedures used in the dissemination process and report on teachers' reactions to it.

Foreign Language Teaching in Bulgaria: The Role of Culture

Bulgaria has a long history of state schools which immerse pupils in a foreign language by delivering most of the curriculum in the FL concerned (Danova, Krusteva-Bossakova and Stoitzov, 1993). The English-medium schools are prestigious and prominent (twenty eight schools and twenty thousand pupils in a country of approximately eight million). The FL classroom has traditionally been seen as a place where pupils learn *about* the language and *about* the people who speak that language. The focus has been gradually changing: linguistically, pupils are now encouraged to communicate in the language, ie a skills focus. A comparable change is possible with regard to the cultural content whereby pupils are encouraged to develop cultural awareness skills. This project is about the development of such skills in the FL classroom.

The Cultural Revolution: from topic-based to skills-based culture teaching

In the last decade, culture teaching has seen dynamic curriculum development (eg. Byram, 1997) especially in central and eastern Europe (eg. Patten, 1995; Cherrington and Davcheva, 1998). These developments argue that:

> ... the provision of information about a country, about the institutions of a society and their history complemented by an intuitive selection of representations of 'everyday life' cannot be the only objective of culture teaching. ... instead [culture teaching] should focus on processes and methods of analysing social practices and their outcomes, thus aiming to provide learners with critical tools and to develop their critical understanding of their own and other societies (Byram, 1997: 19).

The Bulgarian Cultural Studies Project

Bulgarian cultural studies activities and the Cultural Studies Network

Bulgaria has hosted two major conferences in cultural studies and intercultural communication (Cherrington and Davcheva, 1998). There is now a Bulgarian Society for British Studies and courses in British Studies are offered at the major universities. Our concern, however, is the Cultural Studies Network (CSN) which was started by FL teachers who shared concerns about language-culture teaching in the increasingly democratic climate of the early nineties. They wanted to explore their concerns, to understand them better and re-shape their practice. There are now about sixty members, mostly teachers of English in English-medium, state secondary schools. The development and achievements of the CSN are beyond the scope of this discussion, but Davcheva (1994) provides a fuller account of this large-scale, teacher-led in-service development.

Training and its dissemination

The University of Strathclyde provided training for these teachers as they introduced cultural awareness in their teaching. The teachers then shared their cultural studies teaching experiences through the CSN by recording their lessons on diary sheets and circulating them to other teachers. A culture of reflective practice developed. For example, one teacher, Iliana Hristova, wrote:

> The most vigorous function of the network proved to be the diary sheets ... I cannot say what makes me feel happier about such lesson exchange: a diary sheet I have just received and found really handy and useful, or a colleague's acknowledgement of a lesson I have produced. Anyway, both seem equally rewarding. ...With each new diary sheet circulated we become more certain that teaching and classroom experience are worth sharing.

The CSN teachers have developed a strong group identity and commitment to making their language-culture teaching more relevant and effective.[3] The value of the impetus created by the teachers was recognised by Head Teachers and this enabled the development of the *Branching Out* syllabus.

The *Branching Out* cultural studies syllabus

Supported by the Bulgarian Ministry of Education and Science, the CSN teachers have produced the syllabus *Branching Out* as a response to the need for '*a more structured approach to cultural teaching and learning ... a source of new ideas and professional insights*' (British Council, 1998: 9-10). The syllabus' aims are in keeping with those proposed elsewhere:

... language learning should lead to insight and increased understanding of the society and culture of speakers of other languages, but also of the learners' own society and culture and the relationship between the two, a cognitive learning process. ... language learning should lead to positive attitudes towards speakers of other languages, an affective change. (Byram and Fleming, 1998: 6)

Thus, the *Branching Out* authors state that the '*goal of teaching Cultural Studies today is to enable students to develop, alongside their linguistic competence, the kind of inter-cultural competence which will provide them with the means to interpret cultures and communicate more success-fully in an inter-cultural context*' (British Council, 1998: 10). The principles, concepts and processes are drawn from anthropology, the ethnography of communication, and cultural studies, and the syllabus focuses on the skills of *critical reading, comparing and contrasting, ethnography,* and *research* because:

...a skills-led syllabus reflects the nature of cultural learning and its aims. It does not merely give information about one target culture or another; it aims at teaching and providing students with the ability to analyse, understand and appreciate cultural diversity. A skills-led syllabus is versatile as it allows the same topics and materials to be used at various levels and in various ways. It thus creates a feeling of freedom and experiment for the teacher and gives students a sense of the process of growth of both cultural and language awareness (British Council, 1998: 13).

Initiating Classroom Research projects to disseminate the Syllabus

The CSN teachers wanted to help other teachers develop the skills needed for implementation. They decided to create a circle of practising FL teachers who, familiar with the syllabus and its rationale, would experiment with its content. The specific aims of the new dissemination stage are to (i) increase teachers' knowledge and pedagogical skills so that they can more effectively develop their students' cultural awareness, and (ii) enable teachers to use *Branching Out* reflectively in their teaching. Two mechanisms have been adopted:

• double training seminars held regionally for FL teachers

• classroom research conducted by the participant teachers and seminar tutors

Double Seminars – Underlying Principles

The dissemination stage has five underlying principles:

- long-term teacher involvement – based on an initiative of the Council for Cultural Co-operation of the Council of Europe which consists of:

   an initial workshop, at which the latest developments in a particular field are presented, discussed and assessed by the participants. At the end of the first workshop an action programme of Research and Development is planned, initiated and implemented over a certain period. The results of these R and D projects are then presented at a follow-up workshop, which evaluates the end products and possibly recommends follow-up action in the field. (Attard, 1996).

- teacher participation – enabling teachers to contribute to and shape the training themselves through participant-centred seminars which view the teachers' experiences of language-culture teaching as a valuable training resource.

- loop input (Woodward, 1991) – the training process becomes part of the seminar content: the seminar is based on the four main cultural learning skills from the syllabus.

- valuing the whole dissemination scheme and its training events – for example, getting Head Teachers to release staff for the weekday seminars.

- standardisation – by producing a trainer's guidebook to support the syllabus authors acting, for the first time, as seminar tutors.

The First Seminar – Structure

This seminar is divided into six sessions spread over two days. It aims to:

- introduce teachers to the *Branching Out* syllabus

- help them identify and plan for a collaborative research area

- provide them with the tools for reflecting on their own practice and that of their collaborating colleagues.

What is Culture? What is Culture Teaching?

Session 1 aims to surface the teachers' existing perceptions of culture and culture teaching. First, participants present an object which has cultural value for them (the range of objects should demonstrate cultural diversity and the ensuing discussion aims to question the myth of a homogeneous national culture). After this, the teachers reflect on culture learning activities they have used and brought with them. They then develop criteria for 'good' culture learning activities which they use to evaluate their materials.

An aperitif (the syllabus taster), an ethnographic lunch, and a digestif (reflection)

In Sessions 2-5, the teachers meet the four syllabus skills through experiential tasks. First, there is a critical reading task focused by questions such as: 'Who wrote the syllabus?' 'What types of text does the syllabus contain?' 'Who is the Syllabus aimed at?' and 'How typical of its genre is the syllabus?'

The focus then moves to ethnography, an important tool for cultural learning in which the researcher tries to enter into a culture of a particular group and to report on its activities and values from the outside. It emphasises the cultural distance that has to be bridged in order to begin understanding another culture and this requires reflection on the culture(s) being researched and on the culture(s) to which the researcher belongs. The main stages of ethnography are outlined as well as the advantages and disadvantages of this method.

The teachers then carry out ethnographic tasks over the lunch which follows. They have to observe a) interactions between themselves, or b) interactions between themselves and the restaurant staff, or c) the conventions of behaviour at table, eating customs, and attitudes to food. They must write field notes guided by questions such as: *What happened? Why? How did I feel about what was happening/what was said? Why?* Using their field notes, they present their findings, reflect on the practice of ethnography and discuss the use of ethnography to promote cultural learning.

An example lesson

In Session 4, the teachers experience a cultural learning lesson (which demonstrates the syllabus skill of *comparing and contrasting*) and then work with a framework for reflecting on it.

Drawing conclusions

The homework tasks consolidate the day's work on the syllabus and prepare for the future. Session 5 (Day 2), in groups, the teachers discuss their conclusions from the homework task and prepare a presentation articulating their thoughts. The tutors collate the main points and link the issues presented to the concrete practical problems the teachers face.

Classroom research preparation (Session 6)

The teachers are asked whether or not they want to pursue the challenges of cultural teaching by participating in small-scale classroom research (CR) projects which they will design and run in the six months before the second seminar. Work on the projects will enable them '*to move from using new professional terminology about their experience – renaming it – to thinking and acting in different ways – reconstructing their classroom teaching*' (Freeman, 1996: 222). For the remainder of the seminar, the teachers (i) form their CR teams, (ii) decide on the theme and goal of their research, (iii) outline their framework and desired outcomes, (iv) elaborate on the phases within their project, and (v) examine the data gathering tools required for peer observation and reflection. During this stage, the teachers experience the fourth culture learning skill – *research*.

Second Seminar – Structure

This aims to:

• provide space for the teachers to present and discuss their CR projects

• encourage them to analyse their role in promoting language-culture teaching

• re-assure them about the worth of their activities and identify ways for them to continue the process of their professional development.

Each team of teachers reports on the aims and objectives of their CR projects, on their progress, on *critical incidents* along the way (about both teachers and students), on their data and its analysis, on their monitoring and evaluating of CR work, and on the evidence of achievement. A note-taking worksheet is used to guide the teachers in the appraisal of their colleagues' attitudes to their CR experiences. This focuses the listener's attention on the way the reporting teacher expresses herself and talks about her experience, and in particular notes the words which relate to (i) the effects (on their ideas, professional behaviour and classroom dynamics) of teaching with the syllabus, (ii) any perceptions of emerging change, and (iii) student responses to the new materials and shift in focus. When everybody has presented, the teachers in groups discuss the impact of the syllabus on the teaching/learning process. In the final seminar session, the teachers weigh up the criticisms of the syllabus against its usefulness and pioneering role in culture education.

Initial Reflections on the first phase of the Dissemination

There have been twenty two implementations of the first seminar and these have been seen as effective and enjoyable. What reasons lie behind this perceived success? What might be the immediate and longer-term effects on the teachers? What factors will help create the pedagogical momentum needed to take the project to its end? Our answers are drawn from (i) first-hand impressions as both tutors and participant-observers on the seminars, (ii) collected seminar records (eg. flipchart sheets) of the teachers' contributions, (iii) informal conversations with teachers and tutors during and after the seminars, and (iv) post-seminar tutor reports, data from feedback questionnaires, and narrative feedback from participants.

Reflections on Seminar 1- Introductory Session

The teachers' objects ranged from tourist-type representations of Bulgarian-ness (eg. embroidery) through personal treasures (eg. jewellery), and on to the unexpected (eg. home-made yoghurt and a pet ferret). Their stories opened up new self-perceptions through which they realised that they shared a teacher identity but now needed to recognise each other as members of different social groups in terms of age, ethnicity, region, gender, and nationality. One teacher writes that the first activity '... *created a friendly atmosphere, team spirit, and stimulated us for new discoveries'*. This helped establish the innovatory aims of the seminar: *'There was absolutely no trace of the usual Bulgarian scepticism, of that typical we've heard-this-all-already attitude'*. The result was an increased awareness of the need to understand what teaching culture involved and to go beyond the easy attraction of isolated facts.

Problems teachers face regarding culture teaching

During this session, the teachers list 'problems' they have experienced when dealing with culture in their classrooms and any concerns they might have about teaching culture in the future. Throughout the seminar the group refer back to this as they try and find some answers. The problems identified fall into four groups:

- external constraints such as lack of sources of information, limited access to quality materials, lack of age-appropriate materials, lack of time, and rigid syllabus

- teaching concerns such as the lack of self-confidence in their language-culture teaching ability, inadequate training received at university, little experience in the target culture, lack of language to talk about and analyse cultures, unachievable aims, difficulty in matching conceptual frameworks in different cultures, and uncertainty about the appropriacy of trying to influence pupil attitudes

- pupil attitudes towards culture learning such as scepticism and indifference, refusal to understand foreign rituals and customs, insufficient language proficiency, the tendency to use the native language and the students' sensitivities related to language, ethnicity, religion, age and lack of information about the foreign culture

- shared teacher-pupil concerns such as the mismatch between pupil and teacher interests, cultural intolerance, persisting stereotypes and prejudices, lack of close contact between cultures and few opportunities to meet native speakers of the target language.

The problems listed convey a mixed picture of teachers' perceptions, ideas and levels of anxiety. The 'target culture' and the provision of information about it loom large. It is conceptualised as an entity separate from the study of language, demanding a place of its own in the already loaded school curriculum. Another perspective reveals it as a matter of developing a whole new way of understanding the roles of teachers and students in approaching the study of language. Thus the session leaves the participants with raised curiosity and well-structured expectations about the questions the seminar and the Syllabus itself will try to address.

Reflections on the ethnography sessions

The introduction to ethnography and observation task (Session 2 plus lunch) have been well-received. While the previous sessions were based on a more familiar diet, the ethnography sessions presented teachers with perceptual and procedural challenges. They found it strange to preoccupy themselves with cultural trivia such as restaurants and the people who ate and worked there; they could hardly see the point since the situation was so commonplace; they struggled to establish adequate distance between themselves and the observed event. However, once over their initial surprise, they carried out the tasks with zeal. Their understanding of the significance of ethnography grew as the observation and reflection processes progressed. Here is one example of fieldnotes made during lunch:

> The seminar participants were given a lunch break and were invited to McDonald's. They went there in small groups of two or three. They ordered their food individually and were seated at different tables. They didn't have the chance to sit together as whole group. Those who managed to find vacant seats first, tried to reserve them for the others. Communication during lunch was entirely in Bulgarian with just an occasional use of English words as opposed to the situation in the seminar room where the same people communicated in English only. The continued use of English at the restaurant would have been embarrassing both to the participants and to the rest of the customers. Close friends and colleagues used the informal way of addressing each other and those who had met for the first time used the polite form. The topics of conversation were rather general – McDonald's, fast food restaurants, their novelty and attraction to Bulgarians and children in particular, the staff's efficiency, different tastes and preferences. The seminar, as a topic of conversation, did not come up, probably because the participants needed a change from the more formal atmosphere of the seminar room. The general feeling that the participants shared was that the fast meals offered at the restaurant do not appeal very much to Bulgarians who are used to a more leisurely way of eating both at home and at traditional restaurants. In spite of that all the seminar participants

enjoyed themselves and the atmosphere at the tables was relaxed and easy. On leaving the restaurant, the group was seen to break up into smokers and non-smokers.

Reflections on the sample lesson

The teachers discussed the lesson from the perspectives of both learners and teachers. Alternating between the two perspectives reminded the teachers that their own views do not necessarily converge with their learners' and that difference, if handled skilfully, could turn into a productive driving force in the classroom. Apart from confirming that the sample lessons in the syllabus work, this session also guided the teachers through the reflective process which is necessary if they are to carry out classroom research projects.

Reflections on the classroom research preparation

Originally planned as a 'dry' planning session, the way this developed took tutors and participants by surprise. The room was ablaze with the excitement of preparing for what were going to be, for most, their first classroom research projects. The novelty of the decisions which needed to be made (formation of teams, choice of themes and agreement on what to research, timing) mingled with a sense of professional responsibility. It was generally felt that classroom research would add a completely different dimension but most probably another burden to their 'normal' school work. In anticipating the demands of their new role, the teachers found it hard to see into the future to structure the experience they imagined going through. And yet, the passion to experiment and develop won the day. The frameworks of the future research projects were eventually drawn and the teachers concluded the first seminar with the knowledge that they would come back to turn the second seminar into an event of their own making – a professional triumph.

Teachers' overall appraisal of the first seminar

Upon completion of the first seminar the participants analyse their own perceptions of new learning. They recognise the fact that the seminar has the potential to revolutionise their understanding of the philosophy of culture teaching:

So far we haven't thought of teaching culture in that way. We tend 'to teach' culture in a way just to transmit information to students rather than expect them to work on their own and come up with their ideas and suggestions. To this effect a skills-led approach is an essential achievement.

Some of the teachers are fascinated by the importance attached to the ability to reflect upon one's own culture:

I understood that you have to help your students become aware of our native culture. It can have so many different interpretations. And all of them are bound to the culture that has produced them and also to the culture that will interpret them.

The teachers have also become aware that culture education involves the definition of a new role for the teacher:

The seminar has made me think that it takes a motivated and an open-minded teacher to teach culture: a guide and a mediator in the process of intercultural learning; a teacher whose students are her partners.

Some of the teachers have come to realise the importance of serious preparation work before undertaking the task of teaching culture:

Doing culture in the classroom is quite challenging. It means a lot of work done beforehand. Do not just do culture for culture's sake. Set clear objectives and aim to develop particular skills. Put more emphasis on interpretation at the expense of factual information.

Conclusion

We await the full results of the classroom research projects but this is what a teacher wrote[4] after she had begun hers:

... I have always been interested in developing intercultural awareness. The Syllabus and the seminar have given me new ideas and an opportunity to improve my thinking and teaching in this direction. Teamwork is a gift. My students and I get to know each other in circumstances different to the ones in the classroom but still connected with learning. The Syllabus creates conditions for that. Initiative, tolerance, respect for others and self-respect – these are key order for us. We have gone a long way to understand that learning does not only happen in the classroom. We've broken free from the constraints of the student-teacher-coursebook triangle and have opened our eyes and ears to people and learning outside the classroom.

The dissemination stage of the cultural studies project is ongoing but already the passion of the teachers, the enthusiasm for the classroom research projects, and the evidence of professional and personal development are being heard. The syllabus will enable teachers and their pupils to culturally branch out only if it continues to take root in this way. We await the fruit that will follow with hopes of a fine harvest.

References

Attard, P. (1996) *Report of workshop 13B, Qawra, Malta*. Graz: European Centre for Modern Languages.

British Council (1998) *Branching Out: A Cultural Studies Syllabus*. Sofia: The British Council.

Byram, M. (1997) *Teaching and Assessing Intercultural Communicative Competence*. Clevedon: Multilingual Matters.

Byram, M. and Fleming, M. (Eds, 1998) *Language Learning in Intercultural Perspective: Approaches through Drama and Ethnography*. Cambridge: Cambridge University Press.

Cherrington, R. and Davcheva, L. (Eds, 1998) *Teaching Towards Intercultural Competence: Conference Proceedings*. Sofia: The British Council, Bulgaria.

Danova, M., Krusteva-Bossakova, L. and Stoitzov, O. (1993) Foreign language education in Bulgaria: present-day situation and future tendencies. In Ager, D., Muskens, G. and Wright, S. (Eds) *Language Education for Intercultural Communication*. Clevedon: Multilingual Matters.

Davcheva, L. (1994) National teacher education seminar, Burgas, November, 1993. *British Studies Now* (January) London: The British Council.

Freeman, D. (1996) Renaming Experience/Reconstructing Practice: Developing New Understandings of Teaching. In Freeman, D. and Richards, J.C. (Eds) *Teacher Learning in Language Teaching*. Cambridge: Cambridge University Press.

Patten, E. (1995) Bucharest: an MA for the future. *British Studies Now*, Issue 5 (January) London: The British Council.

Woodward, T. (1991) *Models and Metaphors in Language Teacher Training*. Cambridge: Cambridge University Press.

Notes

1. In the 1980s and 1990s, there was some dissatisfaction within FL teaching circles (especially in Europe) regarding the 'culture-free' orientation of communicative methodology. Teachers wanted the communicative thrust of recent methodology to be linked to a concern with pupils being able to communicate with other people (ie 'natives') in the foreign language. FL teaching has thus become associated with cultural studies teaching and the language classroom potentially has become a site for developing what is variously termed cultural awareness, intercultural competence, cross-cultural capability, and even a sense of European citizenship or identity. With

regard to EFL teaching, this drive towards a re-integration of language teaching with cultural teaching proved particularly popular in eastern and central Europe where British Studies, or sometimes British Cultural Studies, often became a curriculum area in its own right. The cultural studies project discussed here should be seen as part of these exciting times.

2. Leah Davcheva provides the insider voice in this chapter as a Bulgarian, a language teacher and teacher educator, and as project director for various cultural studies projects. Richard Fay provides an outsider perspective having become involved in an advisory capacity in the project as a result of supervising the dissertation of Keith Kelly, a Manchester MEd student and member of the cultural studies project. We hope that our collaboration will continue to be productive during the next stage when distance learning materials (dealing with cultural studies for language teachers) will be written.

3. In addition to the intensive training they received, the teachers committed themselves to sharing their teaching experiences by circulating the lesson records, diary sheets, to all the schools involved. In the process, the CSN members developed a sense of belonging to a group whose mission it was to work towards more relevant and effective culture teaching. An early expression of their sense of group identity was the newsletter, *NetNews*.

4. Personal communication to Leah Davcheva.

PART 3: Collaboration across boundaries

CHAPTER NINE

Teacher education for teachers of English and French:
developing parallel distance learning programmes in Greece

Richard Fay
University of Manchester

Julia-Athena Spinthourakis
University of Patras

Marie-Christine Anastassiadi
University of Athens

Introduction

Two Countries, Two Universities, Three Programmes, and One Set of Materials

Our story is about the birth of a new university, about the transplant of distance learning materials which has aided its early growth, and about our search for an appropriate distance learning methodology. We begin with the emergence of our collaboration.[1]

Talking in the heat (from Richard's Diary)[2]

[June 1996] After a bakingly hot day, it is a relief to be in the air-conditioned top-floor suite of the Ministry of Education in central Athens. Turning from the plate-glass windows overlooking the Acropolis, the Minister[3] enquires: 'What else is needed for the collaboration to go ahead?' 'Just discussion of the details'. Next day: thank God for the recuperative powers of ouzo – we've just had six hours of discussion, the first four were fine agreeing the academic and organisational part, but when we came to the financial and contractual part, the air-conditioning went off – one way to speed things up I guess. Anyway, the deal is done, and we can now start in earnest.

[June 1997] It's already too hot for me at nine in the morning. I stupidly decide to catch the bus to meet Professor Sophia Papaefthymiou-Lytra[4] at the University of Athens. Taking the suitcase with 15kg of distance learning materials doesn't help and the struggle to the 9th floor office makes me wonder just how hard this project is going to be.

[June 1998] We are in a rented educational building in the northern suburbs of Athens on a quiet Saturday morning. 'We' means the four Athens-based tutors, their students for the first half-modules, and a few materials writers for the French programme. I feel really optimistic: the first contact session of the first module of the first cohort on the first full programme of the HOU which is itself a first, being the only open and distance learning public institution in Greece. Watching the students, they seem familiar yet different from ours. Watching the tutors, I'm impressed by their professionalism; it's all new for them, and I wonder how they can project such confidence – it must be hard to 'own' the materials and also fit into a new academic culture which has yet to crystallise into something tangible. And watching the French writers whose focus has been on content, I wonder how they feel actually seeing students working from parallel materials. I also feel a sense of doubt – will our materials work here? Will the tutors like them and use them effectively? Will the problems be so glaring that we lose face? I feel like my head is on the block but I guess everyone is feeling stressed out by the situation – it's new for all of us.

[June 1999]. The writing team (for this chapter) are sitting in a cafe in the Plateia in Thesio in touching distance of the Acropolis. It's dusk but still too hot for comfort. We begin talking. At first, people are a bit reticent and I lead by rehearsing the kinds of questions I have in my mind. Then the ideas flow quickly, the anecdotes told, the questions raised. It becomes more a question of managing the flow than of stimulating it.

The Project

The HOU development provides our overall but still emerging context. Within this, we focus on the development of the programme for teachers of EFL and the transplant of distance learning materials from the University of Manchester to the HOU.[5] The materials are being used without change for one programme (for teachers of EFL) and as a point of departure for the materials writers for another programme (for teachers of FFL).

The story is complicated because the newness of the HOU means that its institutional culture and constituent programme cultures are still emerging. We are interested in what happens when materials are transplanted in this way and in the influences which help new academic cultures emerge; in brief, in what provides *appropriate methodology* (Holliday, 1994) for these programmes. We focus on the questions which need to be asked if this goal is to be reached, and present some initial perceptions about the transplant.

The Hellenic Open University

Some development factors

In December 1997, the HOU was founded as the 19th Greek university (Lionarakis, 1996), the first to specialise in distance learning as a teaching/learning methodology. DL makes good logistical sense given the scattered islands and the thinly-populated countryside of modern Greece. It also makes good educational sense. Many Greeks want their children to complete higher education. The existing universities have had difficulty in meeting the demand created by such aspirations and many young people therefore study overseas. The HOU will help meet the high demand for HE as well as restore the balance between home and foreign degrees.

An intentionally innovative open/distance learning university

As a campus-less university, all programmes are offered by DL coupled with face-to-face and telephone sessions. To broaden the provision available, especially at post-graduate level, the HOU's programmes are consciously innovative. Thus, although Masters programmes in Applied Linguistics and Translation exist (at the University of Thessaloniki and the University of Athens respectively), the HOU's provision for language teachers is unique. The programme for EFL teachers began in June 1998. In January 2000, the second wave of new programmes will be launched and the aim is to offer over 20 programmes by the year 2002. Of these, the most interesting here is the programme for French (FFL) teachers.

Teacher Education for Foreign Language Teachers in Greece

Until recently, the main emphasis of the undergraduate programmes in English and French philology offered by the 'traditional' universities has been on language, linguistics, and literature, and only secondarily on training language teachers. However, in recent years, universities have expanded their courses for students intending to teach EFL and FFL. Many of the teachers taking HOU programmes probably graduated before the recent innovations.

Current practice in the preparation of teachers of FFL involves a four-year course at the University of Athens or of Thessaloniki. In the final year, students follow a methodology course and carry out observation in a state secondary school. During their observation period they teach at least one lesson. They are not obliged to spend a period in France. The situation is similar with regard to the initial training of teachers of EFL. This requires some observation of state school teachers and may provide some small-scale 'teaching'. During their studies, students make presentations on what they would do in the classroom. Additionally, students complete a short supervised teaching practicum. Overall, the result tends to favour theory over practice.

In the past, after graduation, many teachers accumulated experience in the private sector as they waited for a post in a public school. It could take up to ten years to find a place in a provincial school. The situation has changed since the 1998 introduction of a national exam to select teachers. Although in-service training exists for both public and sectors, until the opening of the HOU programme, there was no Masters-level course for those wishing to specialise in language teaching.

Collaboration

A Greek affair

The HOU's programme for EFL teachers is administered by HOU officers and coordinated by the HOU Academic Responsible. It is taught by HOU tutors and culminates in an HOU award. Students are drawn from Greece and their work is assessed by HOU tutors. The HOU functions as a public Greek university and its academic quality is monitored according to Greek norms. Although the HOU has embraced support from elsewhere, and although many of its participants, both tutors and students, have significant experience of other educational cultures, the HOU is an avowedly Greek affair. However, the HOU, as an open university, must find a balance between the philosophical orientation of distance learning and that of the 'traditional' university sector in Greece. The flexibility and learner-centredness of distance learning may prove to be key areas in this search.

Transplanted courseware, diverse cultural influences, and emergent cultures

The courseware was originally written for an international student body, according to the norms of CELSE's educational culture and models of teacher education and distance learning. The transplant context is an 'emergent culture' (Holliday, 1999) in which diverse cultural influences are at play: these include institutionalised cultures, methodological cultures, the culture of the materials, and participant cultures. If this emergent culture is to be successful, its way of working needs to be appropriate to that context (see Fay and Walsh, 1996).

The picture is further enriched as the transplant materials have also been used as a resource in the development of the materials for the programme for FFL teachers.[6] Once this programme commences, a related emergent culture will develop. Just how similar this will be to that of the EFL programme remains, as yet, a fascinating unknown. However, we are already speculating about the influence that may result from differences in EFL and FFL methodology, and from different attitudes regarding teacher education in those two language teaching specialisms. Marie-Christine notes that '*comparé au matériel anglais, le contenu des livrets français est plus théorique, l'approche y est diachronique, plus conforme à la bibliographie française*' [compared to the English materials, the French modules are more theoretical; the approach is chronological conforming to the French rhetorical tradition].

The HOU's programme for EFL teachers follows a bottom-up approach. It begins with the materials for the four skills, then moves through the areas of assessment and course design, and concludes with electives in young learners, educational technology, and possibly intercultural communication, ESP, grammar, and teacher education. By comparison, the programme for teachers of FFL adopts a top-down approach. It begins with course design (to provide a clear map of the overall scheme of things) and then looks at specific areas within this. It has no electives (a funding constraint rather than a design consideration) but places inter-cultural and technological considerations in its core provision.

The issue of culturally-sensitive collaborations is very important. Materials providers have experience in their field but if the transplant is to avoid tissue rejection then the collaboration needs to develop into something mutually beneficial. Julia-Athena comments that

> while the HOU is still in its infancy and should continue to have Manchester as its mentor, we shouldn't neglect the fact that Manchester can learn from the experiences of the HOU. In this way Manchester can also adapt its own internal program practices and modules to meet the diverse needs of its expanding worldwide clientele.

Types of Collaboration

The task we are involved in, that of gaining a deeper understanding of appropriate methodology in DL mode teacher education across language specialisms, is a large one. It can be usefully broken down by considering the different types of collaboration which the project is producing. The main types are between:

- EFL methodologists (from Britain and from Greece) and metho-dologists (from Greece and France)

- EFL teachers and their HOU tutors, and FFL teachers and their HOU materials writers

- EFL teachers in Greece who belong to different teaching sectors and are part of the HOU's emergent programme community

- Distance learning methodologists and subject area specialists.

The search for appropriate methodology and the questions we need to ask

By researching the three programmes (ie Manchester's programme for EFL teachers, and the HOU's programmes for teachers of EFL and FFL), we believe that insights can be gained of relevance to DL methodologists and providers. We have generated the following questions:

- What methodological assumptions should the design of the DL materials be based on?

- Are they equally appropriate from one national context to another?

- Do DL methodologists from the Anglo-Saxon school[7] and those working within higher education in Greece share a sense of what is appropriate DL methodology?

- What happens when DL materials are transplanted from one educational context to another? Where/why is modification needed?

- Do tutors feel a lesser sense of course ownership if they use transplanted courseware rather than writing their own?

- How easy is it for tutors and students in Greece to embrace the DL methodology?

- What challenges (eg. regarding assessment) does DL present in Britain and in Greece?

- How do the tutor-teacher relationships change when the mode of study is DL rather than face to face institution-centred provision?

We next present some insights gathered from materials writers, tutors and students.

Initial perceptions

Materials design

The French team have written their own materials. They have been doing this while the English team has been implementing the transplant materials. Marie-Christine reflects on the differences:

> Le concept d'enseignement à distance est inconnu jusqu'ici. Certains éléments qui existent dans les livrets (par example, les questions d'auto-évaluation) sont nouveaux pour la réalité grecque. [The concept of distance learning is quite unknown. Certain features in the units (for example, the self-evaluation questions) are new to the Greek situation.]

She goes on to reflect positively on this very feature:

Pour des enseignants habitués à faire cours en classe, il est assez difficile d'écrire sans avoir son public en face, en devant imaginer à chaque fois ses réactions. On écrit pour un public qui est encore virtuel (on ne connaît avec certitude ni son parcours, ni ses demandes) très présent par son absence. Ce sont les QAE et les activités qui, à mon avis, posent le problème le plus intéressant. Les consignes doivent être claires et concises pour faciliter la tâche des étudiants

[It is difficult to write without your students in front of you. You have to keep imagining their reactions. You are writing for a virtual audience (we don't know for certain what their experience or their needs are) very present by its absence. Writing the SAQs (self-assessment questions) is the most interesting problem. Rubrics have to be clear and concise to aid the students' task]

It will not be until the French materials are used, however, that we will know whether the transplant has been successful.

For the English tutors, Julia-Athena notes that the English materials present a balance of theory and practice. Theoretical grounding is provided in the relevant module subject area as well as the opportunity for the teacher to assess how well they understand theory through the SAQs. The philosophy of the HOU programme (as demonstrated in the practically-oriented assignments as well as in the theory-in-the-service-of-practice input materials) gives experienced EFL teachers the opportunity to immediately implement their new learning in their teaching. (See Figure 1). This encourages them to structure their assignments according to the needs of their context. It also asks them to be responsible for their own learning, to become classroom researchers rather than consumers of second-hand wisdom.

Appropriateness

In deciding how appropriate the HOU programmes are for language teachers in Greece, we considered why teachers would want to take the programmes. Since the French team have yet to enrol actual students, let us focus on Julia-Athena's experience of the English programme. The students are predominantly female, aged from their late twenties to late forties, – all graduates of English Philology. They are highly motivated

---

Figure 1: Comments from HOU Students taking the Reading/Writing module

'How am I supposed to prepare a reading lesson when I am a **language** teacher'.

'I have my students work in mixed ability pairs or small groups because I **think** or it **feels** like it's the right thing to do'.

'The Ministry of Education curriculum guidelines say to start this lesson with these tasks and therefore I do it'.

'I always used to include a reading aloud exercise in my English classes, I didn't know that the long-term benefits of this practice were limited, at best. I didn't realise what it did to my weaker students' self-esteem to have them read aloud'.

'**Now** I know what I have been doing is using Schemata Theory'.

'Oh my God, I didn't realise how much talking I did in the classroom, I barely gave time to my students to express their thoughts'.

---

albeit perhaps naive about the time required for their studies. They teach in diverse contexts (elementary, middle, and high schools; foreign language schools; tertiary vocational and technical schools; and university foreign language institutes) and this diversity makes for interesting assignments and discussions in the contact sessions. Their desire to study is repeatedly articulated in terms of a desire to become better at what they do. The needs of this highly motivated student body need to be understood in terms of their readiness for the communicative thrust of the HOU's programmes. Here we can gain insights from the French team:

> Au cours de leur formation universitaire, les étudiants sont déjà initiés à l'approche communicative à travers les cours de didactique et les observations de classe. Dans le cadre de l'enseignement dans des établissements publics du secondaire, l'application des méthodes d'enseignement/apprentissage communicatif apparaît plus complexe à cause: a) de l'hétérogénéite des niveaux des apprenants; b) du nombre restreint d'heures de cours (deux heures par semaine); et c) du type d'évaluation (sommative et non formative). Les enseignants ont donc recours à une pédagogie différenciée et adaptent les principes de l'approche communicative à leur réalité de travail.

[Students are introduced to the communicative approach during their university training but in the state schools application is complicated because of the mixed levels of the learners, the limited number of hours (two per week) and the summative rather than formative assessment procedures. Teachers vary their teaching and adapt the principles of the communicative approach to the realities of their situation.]

Further insights come from the feedback the English teachers give us.

The comments reveal some early frustration but also an appreciation for a rigorous methodological grounding and for an informed understanding of what currently happens in their classrooms. One of the teachers, Stavroula Lagou, recently (1999) published an article in the professional EFL newspaper in Greece. She comments favourably on being asked to provide feedback:

The HOU's innovatory strength was once more portrayed when, on completion of our first year of studies, the university personnel asked postgraduate students to complete an evaluation form concerning both the program and the tutors. This ... proves that the people there do care about the quality of the material and the scientific efficiency of the academic staff. Suggestions about further development of the material, as well as various alterations students might propose are also welcome.

Assessment

In the programme for EFL teachers, the assignment load used at CELSE has been supplemented with mini-assignments and a viva voce exam for each module. For most tutors the move away from the 'traditional' university approach to assessment is a move into the unknown. It has involved the creation of detailed analytical descriptors for specified assessment criteria as well as written feedback on the students' work, and standardisation to increase inter-tutor reliability.

Julia-Athena comments too on important tutor perceptions on the assessment procedures.

Assessment is an issue vital to any learning endeavour. One of the first things we did as tutors was to go through an introductory assessment training process. We discussed criteria, graded papers and discussed our conclusions as a group, all in an effort to develop inter-rater reliability standards. The Academic Responsible collects examples of our assessments of students' 'best' and 'worst' efforts to use as assessment training documents. Within the DL process, assessing a student assignment is a time-consuming and difficult process, sometimes taking three hours. It isn't merely a matter of coming up with a grade but requires our being able to give the student relevant comments that lead towards the desired goal. Manchester's assessment training seminar[8] gave us the opportunity to revisit and refine our assessment criteria to aid in the more efficient and effective assessment of student assignments. Assessment is an ongoing process.

Conclusions

The creation of the HOU is a huge development and represents a brave step into a future where distance learning is an accepted part of the Greek HE context. It carries with it the aspirations of hundreds of language teachers and its parallel programme development provides a special opportunity to assess the practices of the different language teaching specialisms as well as assess the needs of those different bodies of teachers. Julia-Athena adds:

> Through the collaboration with Manchester, we have had the opportunity to reflect critically on the design and philosophy underpinning distance learning and the appropriacy of that learning mode according to varying contexts. Already, from the comments of students, tutors, materials writers, and transplant consultants, we are seeing a wealth of data being produced. As the HOU's educational culture establishes itself in coming years, we will have the potential for researching the many questions which this chapter has raised.

Acknowledgements

In the writing of this chapter, many people have willingly opened up their perspectives for us and in particular we must thank the Academic Responsible, Dr Sophia Papaefthymiou-Lytra. In addition, we wish to thank all the tutors, and especially Dr Anastasia Papakonstandinou and Dr Adonis Taglides, who welcomed outside observers into their sessions. Without such support, our efforts to narrate this collaboration would be much impoverished.

References

Fay, R. and Walsh, G. (1996) Some Intercultural Perspectives on Distance Education. In Motteram, G., Walsh, G. and West, R. (Eds) *Distance Education for Language Teachers. Proceedings of the 2nd Distance Learning Symposium* Manchester: University of Manchester, pp. 73-85.

Holliday, A. (1994) *Appropriate Methodology and Social Context*. Cambridge: Cambridge University Press.

Holliday, A. (1999) Small Cultures. *Applied Linguistics* 20/2: 237-264.

Lagou, S. (1999) Distant Learning in Greece *ELT News* No. 127 (September), pp 18 and 21.

Lionarakis, A. (1996) The Establishment of the Hellenic Open University. *Open Learning* 11/3: 53-59.

Notes

1. This chapter has been written by representatives of the three programmes, each writer bringing diverse cultural influences: Marie-Christine Anastassiadi (Greek-French, materials writer for the HOU's programme for teachers of FFL); Richard Fay (Anglo-Irish, Course Director for Manchester's programme for teachers of EFL); and Julia-Athena Spinthourakis (Greek-American, tutor for the HOU programme for EFL teachers). In the initial discussion stages, Moira Hill (Anglo-Greek, Manchester alumnus and tutor for the HOU programme for EFL teachers) made important contributions. We hope that our writing has been infused with this cultural diversity as well as by our multiple professional roles.

2. Richard Fay has been responsible at Manchester for negotiating the contract and overseeing the collaboration with the HOU. These introductory memories form part of his ongoing participant-observations of the developing HOU and its emergent programme cultures.

3. George Papandreou was then Education Minister in the PASOK government.

4. Dr Papaefthymiou-Lytra of the University of Athens English Department specialises in EFL methodology amongst other things and is the Academic Responsible for the HOU's programme for EFL teachers.

5. The materials concerned have been developed for CELSE's MEd in ELT programme. To date, six modules have been licensed to the HOU:

   • Language Learning Skills and Materials (Reading and Writing)

   • Language Learning Skills and Materials (Listening and Speaking)

   • Assessment in Language Learning

   • Course Design and Evaluation in Language Learning

   • Teaching English to Young Learners

   • Educational Technology for Language Learning

6. The HOU's programme for FFL teachers (or 'Français Langue Etrangère' (FLE) as it is entitled in French) will have six modules:

   Planification des Programmes d'Enseignement et de Cours
   Développement des Compétences Orales
   Développement des Compétences Ecrites
   Nouvelles Technologies et Enseignement du FLE
   Education Interculturelle et Enseignement du FLE
   Didactique de la Phonétique

7. This Anglo-Saxon school might be characterised as task-based and interactive, learner-centred with tutors as facilitators, and oriented towards critical thinking and independent learning. The label 'Anglo-Saxon school' is perhaps a lazy shorthand to suggest that theorising and development of DL methodology has seen significant input in Australia, North America, and Britain and relatively little in Greece for example. The term consciously echoes Holliday's (1994) discussion of the different inputs in EFL theorising. His arguments for a an EFL methodology appropriate to social context are analogous to those we suggest for a DL methodology which is similarly appropriate to its social context

8. Given by Jane Andrews.

CHAPTER TEN

Distance mode INSET as personal change: unfreezing in Russia

Charlotte Woods
University of Manchester

Teresa O'Brien
University of Manchester

Radislav Millrood
Tambov State University

Patrick Andrews
University of Manchester

Introduction

This chapter tells the story of an unusual project in Tambov State, Russia. The writers reflect on their experiences, exploring a model for describing the process of personal change in order to structure their research findings. The model suggests that personal change often occurs in three phases: *unfreezing, changing*, and *re-freezing*. Four voices are heard: those of Radislav Millrood (RM) an experienced Russian teacher trainer, Charlotte Woods (CW) and Teresa O'Brien (TOB), who have worked on the project from the beginning in Russia and Manchester, and of Patrick Andrews (PA), who has co-ordinated much of the work in Manchester.

We have chosen to focus on personal change as we consider that teaching as an activity is very much bound up with an individual's identity or view of self. A teacher's professional practice will be shaped partly by *unconscious* beliefs and attitudes (Everard and Morris, 1996:220). Significant change in teaching practice will involve 'deep' level shifts in values and beliefs. Much of the literature on managing change deals with change at the organisational or group level. Our search for a model of *individual* change led us to the work of Bennis *et al* (1973) in the social psychology literature. Their framework is concerned particularly with change through interpersonal relationships; this seemed important for a project which depended in its early stages on successful work between *outsiders* and *insiders*.

Background – The Tambov Project

The Tambov project is an ambitious British Council (BC) funded in-service training project in its third year at the time of writing. The aim is to support teachers in introducing more communicative methods of English Language Teaching (ELT) in state sector secondary schools in line with new Federal standards. Russia is a vast country and distance education offers opportunities to reach both newly qualified and experienced teachers in smaller cities, towns and rural areas. Tambov City and State were chosen for a pilot project because of their relative proximity to the Moscow BC office (about 250 miles away) and because the city has a pool of committed teachers and in particular a Professor of English (RM) who is extremely interested in pedagogy. Figure 1 shows the phases of the project.

Figure 1 shows that teachers were asked to move very quickly from an experience of learning through distance materials, to the experience of writing distance-mode materials for others. Approximately eighty teachers have been touched by the project in some way. About thirty of these have been involved in materials writing and piloting of some kind. The account we give here is necessarily selective and is based on documents and videotapes produced by various stakeholders at various stages of the project.

Describing personal change – the Bennis et al model

The model we have chosen emphasises change through interpersonal relationships and although the literature focuses on the 'change target' (in our case the teachers), we have scrutinised the model in relation to the 'change agents' as well . As fairly experienced teacher educators we expected, and hoped, that the experience we were about to undergo would change us in some way.

Date	Place	Activity
Stage 1 Jan. 1997	Tambov City	2-week introductory course delivered by TOB and CW using specially prepared distance materials on Teaching Listening, Speaking, Reading and Writing and on the Teaching of Vocabulary.
Stage 2 Feb-May 1997	Tambov City	On their own, teachers complete work on the distance materials and classroom research tasks set especially for them. The tasks include videotaping one of their lessons.
Stage 3 June 1997	Tambov City	2 week course led by TOB and CW on writing teaching materials and distance teacher development materials.
Stage 4 March 1998	Manchester	4 week course co-ordinated by PA. Participation in some parts of CELSE's M.Ed programme; distance materials writing for a localised version. CELSE edits, types and prints the materials in preparation for Stage 5.
Stage 5 May-June 1998	Tambov City and Michurinsk	One workshop in each city with the objective of inducting local tutors into teacher development work with two new groups of teachers. CW and TOB work with local tutors (RM and others). Newly prepared localised materials are used.
Stage 5a	Tambov City and Michurinsk	Local tutors manage the marking and feedback of work done by new teachers.
Stage 6 March 1999	Manchester	2-week course and writing workshop for a new group of local tutors. Co-ordinating by PA and CW.
Stage 6a October 1999 on	Manchester and Tambov	Senior professionals begin work on Manchester M.Ed by distance mode.

Figure 1: Phases of Tambov Region Project

This chapter gives a brief overview of the three stages that Bennis *et al* (1973) propose in their model: *unfreezing, changing and re-freezing*. We give examples of how these shed light on our own activities as educators and on those of the participants. Finally, we draw some tentative conclusions about the usefulness of the framework for others working in education.

Phase One: Unfreezing

Experience teaches us that if we want to learn something new, we may have to 'unlearn' something first. Before change can take place, something needs to happen that disturbs the equilibrium of our existing attitudes or behaviour. It is this disturbance that turns our solid beliefs and perceptions into the more fluid state that Bennis *et al* refer to as *unfreezing*. They suggest that unfreezing comes about through three interrelated mechanisms:

- lack of confirmation or disconfirmation

- guilt anxiety

- creation of psychological safety

These are explained below with examples from the project.

Lack of confirmation or disconfirmation

Unfreezing can be triggered when information from our environment tells us that our view of ourselves, or of our situation, is in some way different from the views of those around us. *Lack of confirmation* occurs when the information or circumstances we need in order to maintain our 'operating self-image' are lacking. One example of lack of this for TOB and CW came from the course participants' reaction to an 'icebreaker' activity[1] we employed on the first day of the course. Teachers we had worked with before had responded favourably to such activities, making us feel successful and powerful in being able to induce a positive, friendly atmosphere. On this occasion, however, the participants seemed to be confused by the activity. This *lack of confirmation* gave cause for serious reflection about what kind of activities would or would not work well over the remainder of the course.

An example of *disconfirmation* comes from the diary summaries the teachers wrote at the end of the first course.

> The first day was very difficult and tense. I was shocked a bit. The fact is that I expected to get acquainted with the latest techniques in modern methodology. But I found out that we were to do not only practical tasks, but also theory. Frankly speaking, I'd forgotten theoretical material and of course, I need some revising of it. (T11)

This teacher had probably been feeling quite confident about her knowledge of methodology and teaching but was suddenly feeling under-confident because she realised she was going to have to call on knowledge which she had thrust to the back of her mind.

RM also reports the problems caused by the lack of a 'common professional language'. His own self-image as a knowledgeable teacher educator was challenged by finding that we used technical terms differently. Our use of 'context dependent' when discussing speaking was associated by him with 'context dependent cognitive style' and led him into a discussion with us which he remembers took 'the class astray'. It was difficult for us to know in advance what associations certain terms would have for the Russian teachers. Language teaching in Russia has its own developed tradition with its own terminology. Trying to understand each other's conceptualisations was an important part of unfreezing for all of us.

Guilt anxiety

Where change requires us to unlearn behaviour or attitudes that we are committed to (teaching behaviours honed through years of experience are good examples of this), it will usually be resisted as it suggests that what we have been doing or believing up to now was in some way inadequate. One response is to reject the suggested changes as invalid ('but-it-would-never-work-in-*my*-classroom'). Alternatively, we may react by accepting the information but feeling some sense of inadequacy in ourselves. Perhaps we have not lived up to our own idealised self-image, or we feel that we have disappointed someone whose opinion we value. The resulting feelings can be described as 'guilt anxiety' and change might take place to reduce or avoid these uncomfortable feelings. We can see a little of this in T11's reaction above. T6 too felt worried:

> The first day was very dense and complicated. To adjust to a person, to new terminology, to get much homework – it was nearly shocking and I was, frankly speaking, depressed.

Although the teachers do not actually speak about feeling guilty, obviously many of them were troubled by their struggles in the early days of the course. Most had never been taught by a native speaker of English and it is possible that many, as senior experienced teachers of English, felt something like guilt at not being able to follow our every word. T2 noted honestly '*It seems to me that I was not bright at our classes this time, because it was my first experience in communicating with English people*'.

Creation of psychological safety

Even where there is a willingness to change, which was most certainly the case in Tambov, actual change may not take place either because the outcomes cannot be predicted or because they are known but unacceptable. Anyone involved in helping people to change may therefore be required to allay fears of the unknown, help cope with the anxiety inherent in the change process and/or make the expected outcome seem less difficult to bear. We were aware of the problems the teachers might be experiencing. At the beginning of the second week, TOB's diary entry reads:

> The afternoon worked well though it is obvious many of the teachers have a long way to go in understanding what a communicative activity is. They are beginning to feel de-skilled so we must be careful to keep their confidence high. (TOB 27.1.99)

It is clear that changing attitudes is a complex process. High disconfirmation or guilt anxiety will cause a person to leave the situation, if they are able. A small minority of the participants had come expecting an English language course, seeing this as a rare opportunity to listen to native speakers of English and improve their oral comprehension skills in English. When they realised that they had misread the situation, when their initial assumptions were *disconfirmed*, they dropped out of the course.

Where there is no option but to stay and 'suffer', people may react to disconfirmation by clinging rigidly to their present beliefs and becoming defensive, but this hardly happened in Tambov. One way of helping the unfreezing process is to raise awareness about some inconsistency between actual behaviour and an individual's image of their behaviour (as happened when we discussed teachers' demonstrations of newly created activities). If psychological safety is low, even slight disconfirmation may appear threatening and the suggested change may be rejected. However, where psychological safety is high, relatively small disconfirmations may begin to trigger change. In a very supportive environment, even disconfirmation from past experience can be explored and contribute to change. Evidence that teachers felt psychologically safe can be seen in the willingness with which they videotaped their lessons for us after the course. They had learnt, we feel, to trust us.

The psychological safety of a supportive learning community where participants are encouraged to take risks is important. Striking the right balance so that a defensive reaction will be avoided but change will be brought about is the challenge for the educator. Our experience and the evidence stored in the teachers' summarised diaries suggests that teachers did feel psychologically safe to venture into new areas. We had no problems when we asked teachers to create and demonstrate activities. The particular circumstances of the opening up of Russia after a prolonged period of isolation from other language educators helped to create the climate for change and probably made the unfreezing happen sooner than it might otherwise have done.

T1 noted:

> I gained *much* useful information here. In my everyday notes I often write about the very useful theoretical knowledge I got (concerning 4 skills and teaching vocabulary and grammar). It was useful for me from the practical point of view as I developed a deeper understanding of the activities design. I've always known it's a very difficult task, but the activities I came across during the course showed the stages of the development of an activity. I hope it will be easier for me now to create exercises of different types though I'm rather inexperienced.

The teacher who had spoken of being depressed (T6) continued:

> But in the course of time things began to clear up and by the end of the week I felt much better... Practice was, no doubt, the most familiar and easier than theory. But I found theory very interesting as well, and think it is and will be of great use.

T7 shows balance in her judgement and like several other teachers mentions the benefits of groupwork:

> The studies themselves deceived my expectation, in a positive sense, I mean, because I expected them to be something like our usual course at the INSET centre... But these studies were not mere improving, we had a presentation of a quite new system of teaching and a new system of distance education. I liked the form in which we had our session – we had much time of group work – and that was very encouraging because many of us, and me, personally would not feel sure if we had only front work or if we had to work personally. The group work encouraged our being active and we got to the topics we were introduced to through practice which was very helpful and made much contribution to our understanding of the system. Of course, we didn't get all the things clear, because of the lack of time, but even what we have is very useful and already enough to fulfil the task we have to do by May.

The Bennis *et al* model gives considerable emphasis to the initial unfreezing stage of the change process. No change will occur without it, regardless of the strategies employed.

Phase two: changing

During unfreezing we realise that something in our perception of ourselves or our situation is wrong and that change is needed. This does not necessarily mean, though, that we know what change is required, or how to go about it. In this sense, unfreezing can be viewed as *becoming receptive to new information* and change is *using new information in re-shaping our view of reality*. 'The first step in the change process, then, is to develop alternate assumptions and beliefs through a process of cognitive redefinition of the situation' (Bennis *et al*, 1973:250).

There are two ways that we acquire information for this redefinition of the situation:

• identifying with people

• scanning the environment for multiple sources of change.

Identifying with people

The model includes two different types of identification, *defensive* and *positive*. *Defensive identification* occurs where participation in a course is non-voluntary and where participants see the course leader not as a person but as a position; it tends to lead to new behaviour which is ritualised, restrictive and narrowing. The Tambov course did not take place under such conditions but rather in those which allow *positive identification* to take place. Neither of the course leaders belonged to the local hierarchy and were therefore more likely to be seen as people rather than positions.[2] On our part we had no wish for participants to uncritically imitate the behaviours we demonstrated but hoped that teachers would be able to localise their new knowledge. We were delighted to find that they did this quite spontaneously, even before we had come to the localisation stage of the project.

> ...I'm interested in methods and techniques of teaching rather than theory. But the involvement in the work, a great deal of SAQs,[3] discussions and the wish to find more and more about teaching communicatively through different speaking activities made the understanding of the project clearer... *But while working I accepted the ideas from the point of view of the teacher and transferred them to my work with the pupils in the class. Sometimes it led to misunderstanding of the tasks.* But on the other hand the tasks of planning a lesson, our group work made me creative and I saw very clearly the stages of this or that activity because at the lessons I use many of the techniques which were offered. *As far as theory is concerned, I discovered its necessity because it helps to choose appropriate techniques at all levels.* (T5)

Bennis *et al* suggest that the most effective models for positive identification are people *in transition* between the two 'worlds': the old and the new. A teacher is more likely to identify positively with a fellow teacher who is beginning to assimilate new ideas and move on, than someone who identifies totally with those ideas. There were various people who fulfilled this role. The most senior was RM who, although a respected leader and teacher educator himself, was willing to become one of the class. His interest and creativity were invaluable.

Scanning

This involves scanning the social environment for relevant information to help us change, using multiple sources rather than just one. Typically this process will predominate when there is no emotional attachment to the change agent. Bennis *et al* (p.254) suggest that 'at the extreme, *scanning* implies attention to the *content* of the message regardless of the person, whereas identification implies attention to the *person* regardless of the content.' It seems plausible that solutions arrived at via scanning will be more likely to fit with our usual behaviour and therefore last longer than those arrived at through identification. Several diary references make it clear that the Tambov teachers used each other as sources of information.

> Each group took part in many discussions and activities. So did ours. We learned something new about our colleagues whom we already know pretty well. I really enjoyed Natasha's 'Letter in a bottle' ... and realised that quite a new approach to four language skills (an integrated one) is necessary. (T4)

Further sources of information emerged during the second stage of the project when teachers completed the distance materials on their own and carried out classroom research tasks including videotaping a lesson. Viewing recordings of their own and others' lessons, and consulting items from the collection of methodology and resource books provided additional information to assist the scanning process.

Phase three: re-freezing

The literatures of change and professional development suggest that change is often short-lived unless efforts are made to maintain it (eg. White *et al*, 1991). If permanent change is desired, the process must include the integration of new beliefs and behaviours with an individual's personality (personal re-integration) and confirmation of them by others in their environment (interpersonal re-integration). Bennis *et al* call this process, perhaps not entirely appropriately, *re-freezing*. Contrary to the connotations of *freezing,* they are not referring to a new static state but to the dynamic process of re-integrating the new with the old.

There are two important factors in personal re-integration. Firstly, as suggested above, when information is self-selected during scanning, the resulting change is more likely to fit with our usual behaviour than change induced via identification. Secondly, opportunities for the adaptation of new ideas and behaviours to the local context will also favour their integration with existing beliefs and behaviours. We were delighted that this process of adaptation happened spontaneously from the outset. In the Manchester stages, the process has been aided by the activity of producing distance materials, both theoretical and practical, for Russian teachers.

Inter-personal re-integration is also known to be highly significant in the durability of change. Where an individual is in the process of changing, the reactions of others are highly important. In the Tambov project, these 'others' were the colleagues and pupils of the project participants. There is clear evidence from teachers' accounts that participants offered a strong support network within and between their places of work, reconfirming the new ideas and behaviours, demonstrating to others how to adapt them to the local context and acting as identification models and sources of information to encourage change in colleagues who had not attended the workshops. In Manchester, the Russian teachers worked with PA on the selection of lesson extracts from the wealth of lesson material recorded by the Tambov teachers in the second stage. This involved their thinking through once again the essentials of the proposed changes.

There is diary evidence that the reactions of colleagues who had not taken part in the workshops were mainly favourable. Similarly, self-observation reports and video recordings of lessons suggest that the learners responded positively to the new activities and approach. These favourable reactions from 'significant others' in the participants' environment would have supported the re-integration process.

Lessons and conclusions

This view of personal change as a three-phase process has implications for educators, in their role as agents of change and for teachers, as targets of change and, in their own classrooms, agents of change. All learning involves change and it is interesting to reflect on how the implications listed in Figure 2 below apply to teachers and pupils just as much as they do to teacher educators and teachers.

The Tambov story is not yet complete but we hope we have shown some of the multi-faceted change process as it takes place. As teacher educators we have a deeper grasp of the concepts of localisation and appropriate methodology and of the length of time necessary for change to occur. RM

Phase	For the change target	For the change agent
All three	All three phases are required for lasting change: teachers need to be ready for change, they need to participate actively in changing beliefs and behaviours, and they need to integrate these changes into their teaching personality. They need to be prepared to learn from sources other than the obvious change agent.	Attention must be paid to all three stages. The conditions for unfreezing must exist, the opportunities for scanning must be provided and reinforcement must be available for the maintenance of change (ideally the change target will not be isolated but will be part of a group). The qualities required for the effective 'unfreezer', 'changer' and 'refreezer' are not the same. Different people will function as key players in the three phases. It is important that all possible change agents are drawn into the process.
Unfreezing	They need to be prepared to suffer some psychological discomfort on the way to change. Where a change agent seems unaware of local conditions, current beliefs and practices, it is important to try to heighten their awareness.	Change agents need to be aware of the discomfort that guilt anxiety and the disconfirmation of deeply held attitudes and beliefs can cause and the importance of psychological safety, for example a supportive classroom where participants feel able to take risks. Trying to understand and take as a starting point the change target's perspective will be less likely to result in high guilt-anxiety and defensiveness or outright rejection.
Changing	They need to recognise that change takes place over time and occurs through a range of activities.	Providing salient information from a variety of sources will support the process of *scanning*. Providing guidance on how to obtain information, providing group tasks that can be engaged in without the presence of the change agent are ways in which the *changing* phase can be extended.
Refreezing	They need to integrate new ideas, attitudes, behaviours by adapting them to their own context. This will involve understanding the principles underpinning techniques, activities etc.	Encouraging understanding rather than imitation will aid the integration process. The change targets will be in a stronger position for adapting or reinventing their own techniques and understanding is more likely to enable personally meaningful and longer term change.

Figure 2: Implications for teacher educators and teachers

is constantly reworking the lectures he gives to his trainees, incorporating new ideas into his own frameworks. He is now producing materials to be disseminated via the internet.[4] Russian teachers have become teacher educators and distance tutors... but that is another story.

References

Bennis, W. G. *et al* (Eds, 1973) *Interpersonal Dynamics*. Illinois: Dorsey Press.

Everard, K.B. and Morris, G. (1996) *Effective School Management*. London: Paul Chapman Publishing.

White, R. *et al* (1991) *Management in English Language Teaching*. Cambridge: Cambridge University Press.

Notes

1. The activity involved three stages, each requiring the participants to work in groups of three asking a small set of basic questions to find out something about their colleagues (eg. name, where they worked, expectations for the workshop).

2. This might have been due partly to the fact that we interacted socially with the participants a great deal outside the classroom.

3. Self assessment questions: these are the tasks within the distance learning materials.

4. >http:\\tsu.mtts-tambov.ru

CHAPTER ELEVEN

Developing links into chain reactions:
the critical role of collaboration in
moving from training to research

Jan Majer
Foreign Language Teacher Training College, Łódź

Gary Motteram
University of Manchester

Donald Sargeant
The British Council

Introduction

This chapter describes the productive relationship between a cluster of foreign language teacher education colleges in Poland and the University of Manchester. Teacher educators and teachers worked collaboratively on a number of linked projects which led to the production of a successful, and still unique, video package for trainee teachers, work on in-service training of primary and secondary school mentors, and small-scale collaborative research between the Manchester trainers and teacher/mentors in the Polish primary/secondary school system. This relationship had an impact on a considerable number of teachers. An important element was the stimulus to less experienced teacher educators to write, present and disseminate their work and eventually to begin their own doctoral research projects. The many teacher educators are represented here by Jan Majer (Polish Link Co-ordinator), Donald Sargeant (the Łódź Regional Teacher Trainer for the British Council) and Gary Motteram (Manchester Link Co-ordinator).

Background

When, following the collapse of Communism at the end of the eighties, the political system changed in Poland, the British Council began work with senior Polish teacher educators to increase the number of English language teachers through the newly instituted foreign language (FL) teacher training colleges. Changes in educational policy had been triggered by international bodies such as the OECD and the World Bank, which advocated that Poland raise the percentages of students entering secondary and tertiary programmes (Komorowska, 1996:4). The new freedom of movement led to a strongly felt need for more teachers of western European languages. Poland had for many years had a successful language programme running in schools, with the emphasis on teaching Russian, but with English as a 'favoured other foreign language'. The new conditions meant that English replaced Russian as the first FL in schools.

Before the early 1990s, qualified FL teachers were recruited almost exclusively from the five-year MA programmes run in the Philology departments of universities. In that system, FL teaching methodology was not a top priority. The students, most of whom entered the programme with a view to finding jobs in translation, interpreting, etc., were given a sophisticated education in subjects such as English or American literature, theoretical, historical or applied linguistics. Upon graduating, they often found that all the job market offered was teaching positions in schools. Still, the numbers of qualified teachers leaving universities could not meet the ambitious quotas of the 1990 reform.

The new teacher training colleges were to run innovative three-year courses, in contrast to the five-year courses in the universities so could supply more teachers more quickly. Clusters of colleges were created around, and linked to, universities. The colleges at the heart of this narrative were grouped around the University of Łódź in western Poland. They were in Łódź itself and in Łowicz, Piotrków Trybulnalski, Płock, Sieradz, and Włocławek. The British Council funded a Regional Teacher Trainer (RTT), and the University of Łódź and CELSE in the School of Education at Manchester University[1] were linked as part of a British Council managed project with three main phases. The project started as Polish **AC**cess to **E**nglish (PACE) in 1990, moved on to the **PRe-IN**service and Continuing Education (PRINCE) in 1992 and finally became Support for

Polish Reform In Teacher Education (SPRITE) in 1998. The project is due to finish in 2000.

Educational change

Educational change is a complex process (see also Chapter Ten). We have found it helpful to structure our thinking with reference to the five key ideas that Fullan (1998:253) suggests need to be borne in mind if change is to be successful:

- There is no panacea or model of change
- Change is a highly personal psychological process
- Resistance and conflict are positively necessary
- Improving relationships is the key to successful change
- Emotion and hope are crucial motivators.

We agree with Fullan that there is no one model of change; it is essential to consider contextual factors. Coleman (1992) has shown how initial ideas about what should happen in a project have not always reflected the needs of the participants. This is often the result of preliminary discussions being held at too high a level resulting in little consultation with the end users. This can lead to dissatisfaction if teachers feel that things are being done *to* them, rather than *with* them. If change is a highly personal psychological process, it will only occur where there is consultation. Our link was almost universally welcomed by the teacher educators in the cluster, there was a great deal of hope, and while there was no resistance to the idea of Łódź-Manchester co-operation, there was healthy and sometimes heated discussion on how it should be implemented and what should constitute the core components of seminars.

Figure 1 on page 140 shows the important elements of the project and how they relate to each other.

Manchester input led, at the end of the first two years, to an agenda determined by the Łódź cluster. Two areas were considered important for the second phase. One was examination reform and the second was teacher training. This chapter focuses on teacher training; examination reform is dealt with in Chapter 14.

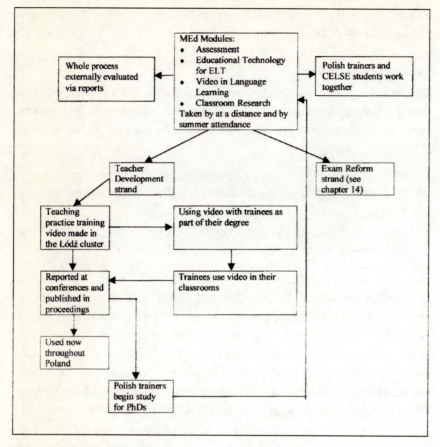

Figure 1: Through collaboration to research

Relationships as the key to successful change

Relationships between many different people had to be developed and we feel that this was facilitated by the very easy and strong relations which held between those of us who were in senior positions. Here, we explore our individual feelings about the project and why we were able to sustain momentum over the full eight years.

Jan—The Link Co-ordinator on the Polish side

At the start of the partnership all the eight links of the PACE/PRINCE project had an equal chance of succeeding, but only some maintained the co-operation with their original partners throughout the eight years of the programme. In the case of the Łótź-Manchester exchange, the key to success was a flexible and pragmatic attitude adopted by both partners.

I firmly believe that the strongest impact of the link at its Polish end was that it created a powerful network of expertise at a time when issues such as young learners, action research, mentoring and teaching practice, for example, were still considered dubious topics in terms of academic inquiry at Polish universities. Thanks to their Manchester link partners, the RTT and academic exchange, the trainers in the cluster felt that what they were doing, both as practitioners and researchers, was not only important and fascinating, but also worthy of study. The PhD projects that have recently emerged under the umbrella of the Support Group represent only a fraction of the universally acknowledged feeling on the part of the trainers that they have participated in a programme which has achieved a major breakthrough in the Polish educational system.

Gary—The Link Co-ordinator from the UK

In the early stages of the Link, I felt quite strongly that the only way that it would develop effectively would be to allow the teachers to make their own choice module when they attended our Summer M.Ed programme. At first, there was confusion about the purpose of the Link and it took some time to clarify this. I think the Link worked effectively because we kept talking about what we needed to do. As far as was possible, given our distance from each other, we worked as a team. Personality also played a role; the core group got on well socially and social meetings were always part of the Link. Donald was important in this respect. Another key aspect of the Link was that all the College teachers were given an opportunity to play a role in the video material that we produced and also in the examination reform. This meant that the younger teachers grew in confidence and were then able to go on and do their own research projects.

Donald – The Regional Teacher Trainer

As a former post-graduate student at Manchester University I was delighted when the British Council chose Manchester to be the academic link for the Łódź cluster. Certainly the links I had formed with the department as a student helped because I was familiar with the Manchester approach to EFL. From the onset I felt that I was part of the team and that it was a co-operative venture both with my colleagues in the Łódź cluster and all the Manchester trainers. The trainers who came were well aware of the difficulties faced by Polish Teacher Trainers at a time when all teachers were forced for economic reasons to have more than one job. Polish teachers worked with dedication and if schedules slipped or agendas changed Manchester trainers showed understanding and flexibility. Undoubtedly, one of the outcomes of the link was the building of strong ties between Polish colleagues in the geographically scattered colleges. The link provided a framework around which the Polish trainers could improve their pedagogic skills while forging academic and personal friendships that continues to nurture future co-operation. It was a pleasure to see how colleagues' methodological skills grew and how they developed the confidence to question approaches and ideas as the project proceeded. I attended nearly all of the Manchester sessions in Poland and was given a warm welcome on my visits to Manchester seeing participants attending modules. It was a learning experience for me both academically and managerially and one which I will remember with appreciation and affection.

Video production and materials production as training for research

The idea of making a teacher education video occurred for several reasons. Firstly, there were very few teacher educators within the college structure with relevant school language teaching experience. Also, many of the overseas teachers working in the system had never seen the inside of a Polish (or any other) school as teachers.[2] The aim therefore was to produce a series of videos that were to be documentary films showing trainee teachers at work with their colleagues, their supervisors and their mentor teachers. Only later did we recognise the research training function of the work. The end result was *Observing Teaching Practice* (Motteram, Sargeant and Majer, 1997), five films which showed whole unedited lessons and, in most cases, pre- or post-teaching interviews.

A task-based training pack was also created, including lesson plans, materials from course books, and feedback from the teacher supervisors and mentor teachers on the filmed lessons. The pack was trialled with groups of trainee teachers. It was created mainly by the Polish teacher educators, along with one representative from Manchester (GM), who had taught modules on *Educational Technology* and *Video and Language Learning* during summer attachments and who acted as advisor. The learning done during these modules has been of great value throughout the project. This is how one of the Polish teacher educators wrote about the experience:

> We graduated from the course with an enthusiasm for film-making and with hands-on experience of the whole process of writing a script, preparing a storyboard, filming and editing. We made ample use of different video filming techniques and learned ways of adapting existing film materials and using them in the classroom. Finally, we followed the whole postproduction process of editing ie going through the process of material selection, preparing a tape log, completing a sound track, deciding about special effects...and characters...The final outcomes were films produced in groups of four – amazing witnesses of group creativity, group dynamics and group stamina to conquer fear of technology and master the use of the equipment. Each of us came home with a video tape of student-produced films and the awareness of what it took to make them. (Lesińska-Gazicka, 1998:79)

Lesińska-Gazicka has since used the same techniques with her own trainees and they in turn have used them with pupils. But, more relevant to the theme of this chapter, the collaborative experience and the confidence were to prove of great use in the training video.

The type of video made was informed by the ideas of Cullen (1991), Laycock and Bunnag (1991) and Wallace (1981), in that it was grounded in the local context and attempted to be as non-interventionist as possible in terms of the disruption of classrooms. Only two cameras were used, one focusing on the teacher trainee and one picking up useful cutaways of the learners. A radio microphone was used to pick up teacher language and a boom to pick up responses from the learners. The camera crew consisted of no more than three people and used natural lighting; the classrooms were not reorganised although space was made so that the boom mike operator and cameras could move around. All the teachers involved in the filming were learning techniques which could be of use to them in later research.

The video was roughly edited in Manchester and then taken back to Poland to be trialled, along with the training pack. This process was time consuming and took several visits before we were happy that we had a pack that was going to serve our purpose. In the process, of course, Polish teacher educators were learning how to do evaluation research. Once the video materials were ready, sixty sets were distributed to all the cluster colleges in Poland and to the INSET co-ordinators.[3]

From training to research

The project has led to several pieces of classroom research. Majer (1998) has analysed the video transcripts in order to make useful points for trainee teachers about teachers monopolising classroom discourse, about trivialised interactions, negotiation of metalinguistic meaning and repair, back-channelling in communicative tasks, excessive use of L1 by students, encouraging initiation of interaction by students, helping students to sustain interaction and enhancing pragmatic and discourse competence. This rich local data has proved invaluable in teacher training.

Andrews, Motteram and Teague (1998) conducted a small scale evaluation of the INSET training sessions for mentors. An interesting finding involved incongruities between the wording of the questions in the structured interview and the teachers' perceptions of themselves and their work. For instance, when asked why they had decided to go into a teaching career, most of the interviewees found the term *career* rather odd. They did not see either the post of teacher or that of mentor as part of a structured career. Another question asked them why they volunteered to become involved in mentoring. The respondents found the verb *volunteer* quite inappropriate. A network of personal and professional friendships and acquaintances provided the infrastructure through which the mentors were approached. The implications of this network suggested that a teacher was unlikely to decline such a request.

The final stage of the project would bear the fruit of a further wave of research projects. As the project continued, it became clear that a number of the college teachers were interested in taking their qualifications further. This was actively encouraged both by the colleges and the British Council. In the final part of the link work, a number of the college teachers came to Manchester on PhD level attachments.

In order to finish this story, we decided to interview each of the PhD candidates, hoping to show the roundedness of the whole project, and the way that the work had impacted on Link tutors in general and these six teacher educators in particular. That they are doing research directly related to work that has come from the Link is an indicator of the success of the project.

A structured interview was used to ask the teacher educators about their developing theses and the impact that the Link project has had on them.

Analysis of the interviews

Topics and type of research

Some limited support for the PhDs is being given by the British Council, and it was agreed at the outset and in the final phase of the PRINCE project that any support for PhD work must be on the understanding that the theses were about teacher education (in its broadest sense) and not about linguistics, or literature, which are very common topics for teacher trainers to pursue in the Polish context. The whole thrust of the Cluster Links has been the improvement of English Language Teaching in Polish primary and secondary schools. The theses are mainly about the teaching of speaking, reading or writing skills, although one is about teacher education itself. All of the participants are doing work that they are calling action or practice-based research, and for most of them this emphasis comes from the module on Classroom Research that they followed in Manchester in the Summer of 1997.

All of the interviewees emphasised the need for networking with others whilst doing a piece of research and pointed to the need for effective support from other colleagues in Poland, from colleagues they met in Manchester, and from tutors. The concept of *critical friends* is one that is advocated strongly on the Classroom Research module. As a direct result of the Link all the college teachers have given presentations at Conferences, some local, some international. They have also begun to produce articles for a variety of publications. The confidence gained from writing and presenting will feed directly into Ph.D writing. In fact, as part of their Polish Ph.D they are required to present and publish before they can begin the formal process of writing their theses.

In response to a question on the impact of the Link on their classroom practice, one of the teachers talked about how the work had enabled her to become a more reflective practitioner. In fact, she felt that she now 'understands the meaning of reflective practice' and is able to apply it to her own teaching. As a result, she has been motivated to encourage her own students to be more reflective. Two others talked about how they had made use of action research in their own classrooms and had seen the transfer of these ideas to their trainees. One specifically reported that her trainees were making use of action research methods in their Diploma projects.

All those interviewed felt that their professional practice had been significantly enhanced by the Link. They pointed most often to their abilities to produce tests and to conduct effective assessment within the Colleges. Two were particularly sure that their confidence to produce tests had been improved by the many sessions that they had attended, but they had also been involved in other professional practice that had come from the Link. One had begun to do mentoring work based on the courses run by the INSET training group; another had been involved in the revision of the reading and writing syllabus and had produced a booklet of integrated reading and writing material which was to be distributed to the rest of the Cluster colleges at the beginning of the next academic year.

Finally, there was a great deal of emphasis on professional contacts. Firstly, at national level, the Links had improved the contact amongst the colleges in Poland itself. But there was also contact with tutors at Manchester and other students from the summer schools. All the respondents stressed that their confidence to do research had been enhanced by seeing that the difficulties faced by teachers in Poland were in fact widespread problems and by dealing with them they could make a difference to the profession as well as themselves.

Conclusions

When the project started, no-one in the Link had research as part of their agenda. It is satisfying to see the way that research questions have emerged slowly out of practice along the lines of the paradigm described by Elliot (1999). It is important that these have emerged from the stakeholders. The Co-ordinators allowed ideas about what was to happen with the Link to bubble up from the Polish trainers and these issues (testing and mentoring) became the focus of the project. As a result, participants have gained in confidence, have learned techniques and have collaborated in training leading to collaboration in research.

References

Andrews, J., Motteram, G. and Teague, J. (1998) Process research: a play in three acts with four characters. In Melia, P.J. (Ed) *Innovations and Outcomes in English Language Teacher Education*. Warsaw: British Council.

Coleman, H. (1992) Moving the goalposts: Project evaluation in practice. In Alderson, J.C. and Beretta, A. (Eds) *Evaluating Second Language Education*. Cambridge: Cambridge University Press p222-246.

Cullen, R. (1991) Video in teacher training: the use of local materials. *English Language Teaching Journal* 45/1:33-42.

Elliott, J. (1999) Evidence-based practice, action research and the professional development of teachers. *Goldsmiths Journal of Education* 2/1: 2-19.

Fullan, M. (1998) Linking change and assessment. In Rea-Dickins, P. and Germaine, K. *Managing Evaluation and Innovation in Language Teaching: Building Bridges*. London: Longman.

Komorowska, H. (1996) Towards quality in teacher education: The contribution of the curriculum. *Proceedings of the PRINCE Link Conference*, Popowo Poland: The British Council. p.3-11.

Laycock, J. and Bunnag, P. (1991) Developing teacher self-awareness: feedback and the uses of video. *English Language Teaching Journal* 45/1:43-53.

Lesińska-Gazicka, A. (1998) Extending the PRINCE link abroad: using video in ELT. In Melia P.J. (Ed) *Innovations and Outcomes in English Language Teacher Education*. Warsaw: British Council. p 75-83.

Majer, J. (1998) Poles apart? Bridging the gap between pedagogic and naturalistic discourse. In Melia P.J. (Ed) *Innovations and Outcomes in English Language Teacher Education*. Warsaw: The British Council. p 145-160.

Majer, J., Motteram, G. and Sargeant, D. (1997) *Observing Teaching Practice*. Warsaw: British Council; Manchester: Manchester University.

Wallace, M. (1981) The use of video in EFL Teacher Training. In *Focus on the Teacher*. ELT Documents 110. London: British Council.

Wallace, M. (1998) *Action Research for Language Teachers*. Cambridge: Cambridge University Press.

Notes

1. Other British universities were linked with other Polish universities and college clusters.

2. The shortage of language teachers had led to the use within the schools of much volunteer teaching organised by bodies such as the Eastern European Partnership (a branch of VSO) and the Peace Corps (USA).

3. Although this material was designed as a training pack for individual teachers, it has also been used in the colleges as part of the regular training for the trainee teachers and as a central aspect of the Łódź cluster mentor training course organised by the INSET co-ordinator. Expertise soon spread. One teacher from Włocławek set up her own mentor courses in her region. Other regions have adopted and adapted the material for their own courses.

CHAPTER TWELVE

The impact of INSET for mainstream teachers in supporting the needs of bilingual pupils

Carol Barnard
Language for Achievement Project, Bolton

John Burgess
University of Manchester

Introduction

This chapter reports on how an in-service programme for mainstream subject teachers helped to meet the needs of bilingual pupils in secondary schools. The programme, funded by a government grant, was offered to secondary teachers in an English urban borough by its language support service. Carol Barnard (CB)[1] a language support teacher working across the curriculum, participated in the design and delivery of the in-service programme with other language support colleagues and with John Burgess (JB), a lecturer specialising in second, foreign and additional language learning at the University of Manchester. Together, we have been researching the impact of the programme and present here an initial analysis of our data.

But first we should explain why the programme was considered necessary. There has long been an unfortunate separation between teachers concerned with the linguistic needs of ethnic minority children and those who conceive of their work in 'subject' terms.[2] While it is obvious to those concerned with language education that language development is an essential element of all learning, it has been difficult to persuade teachers of science, history, geography etc that knowledge about language and language development should be an essential component of their professional competence.

However, the development of English as an Additional Language (EAL) support provision, particularly in classes where a language support teacher works in partnership with the mainstream teacher, has been an important influence on the practices of mainstream teachers, as evidenced in the Partnership Teaching training pack by Bourne and McPake (1991). The in-service programme described here was an extension of this influence: it was a further attempt to develop whole-class teaching strategies and school policies which would address the needs of developing bilingual pupils at the same time as addressing aspects of all pupils' access to the curriculum.

The programme

The programme ran from 1995 to 1998. Figure 1 shows the purpose of the different courses and the participants.

The mainstream teachers, some of whom were heads of department, were drawn from the following subject areas: Maths, Science, English, Modern Foreign Languages, Music, Craft, Design and Technology, Information Technology, Geography, History and Religious Studies. The language support staff were invited in order to

- share their knowledge of the pupils with whom they worked

- maximise their opportunities to develop appropriate strategies

- examine and apply pedagogic theories and methodologies that might be new to them, given that many had come from a mainstream teaching background.

Courses 1 and 2 had two main components, the first dealing with background matters, and the second with methodology, as outlined below.

1. The cultural, linguistic and educational backgrounds of developing-bilingual pupils in the borough:

   • home languages
   • literacy skills of pupils (particularly new arrivals)
   • cultural and religious heritage and orientation
   • introduction to bilingualism
   • role of the language support service

	principally for schools with significant numbers of developing bilingual pupils receiving language support	principally for schools with insignificant numbers of developing bilingual pupils receiving language support
95-6	**Course 1** topics: (i) cultural, linguistic, educational aspects (ii) "common codes" LAC pedagogical approach schools: 4 mainstream teachers: 20 lang support staff: 10	-
96-7	→ → → → →	**Course 2** topics: as in Course 1 schools: 5 mainstream teachers: 10 lang support staff: 3
97-8	**Course 3** Topic: dissemination (mainstream teachers)	-

Figure 1: The secondary INSET programmes in the borough

This component was planned and delivered by members of the language support service, including CB.

2. A 'common codes' Language Across the Curriculum (LAC) approach to teaching mainstream subjects (Burgess and Carter, 1996), designed to facilitate the language development of all pupils through a focus on the language of education and on bilingual pupils' development. Figure 2 shows the conceptual framework of this approach.

The first point to note is that the framework focuses entirely on the 'ideational' or information-carrying function of language (see Lock, 1996 for an accessible account). This, of course, is the language of textbooks, of teacher explanations and of students' essays and examination answers. Starting from spoken or written input, the teacher helps the learners to perceive the organisation of information in a text through carefully focused listening or reading tasks. Visual representations are then used to help the learners produce their own spoken or written discourse. The teachers were introduced to the framework experientially; they worked their way through tasks based on classroom materials. Several important pedagogical principles were emphasised as we worked. They are collected under six overall headings and elaborated below.

Language across the curriculum

•   language for access to the curriculum

Language is an important medium through which all pupils learn all subjects, and is associated with the practice of all skills, across the curriculum. If the main language of the curriculum is one that is additional to a pupil's home/community language(s), as in the case of developing bilingual pupils, there will be a need to develop use of that language to gain full access to the curriculum. Similarly, if the home/community language is a non-standard variety of English, pupils will need to develop their use of standard English as it is used in the curriculum.

•   curriculum as medium for language development

Given the above argument, the curriculum is the best medium through which to develop pupils' use of language. This might go without saying, but it runs counter to the now largely outmoded practice of withdrawing

Input material: spoken discourse and/or written texts	→	Processing	→	"Ideational frameworks"	→	Visual representations	→	Output material: spoken discourse and/or written texts
Listening and/or Reading	→	Thinking, speaking & writing in pairs or groups	→	Organising information in grids, flow diagrams, tree diagrams, according to "discourse types" in input	→	Labelling or completing graphs, maps, pictures; carrying out experiments; etc	→	Speaking and/or writing re input topic or similar

Figure 2: An integrated model: 'common codes' for language development and support of developing bilingual pupils across the curriculum

developing bilingual pupils from mainstream education. Conversely it is the reason for supporting such pupils' learning in the mainstream curriculum. This can be aided by the sort of training our courses offered, and through language support teachers working in partnerships alongside mainstream teachers, as recommended by Bourne and McPake (1991) and Burgess and Carter (1996).

• development of whole-school policy and practice, or practice and policy within specific sectors of the school

Ideally, there should be top-down management support for such approaches, and one effective way to develop this may be to discuss and agree on policies and practices across the school; these may then be written as a code of practice. A step towards this is often the development of policies and practices within departments or faculties.

Integrated pedagogic model

• linkage between receptive and productive skills

In education, as in the real world, we often use the receptive skills of listening and reading, and the productive skills of speaking and writing, in very close relationships to each other, or even sometimes simultaneously. A supportive pedagogic approach is one which gives practice to as many of these skills as possible in association with one body of information (see Figure 2). So in a Humanities lesson on the rain cycle we might get the learners to make notes from a written text, make more notes while listening to spoken discourse – perhaps a video – and then use the notes to practise speaking about the rain cycle before they write it up in an extended text of their own.

• usefulness of 'ideational frameworks'

As an intermediary between reading/listening activities and the speaking/ writing activities, devices like flow diagrams, grids and tree diagrams are useful ways of organising notes. They also provide opportunities for pupils to notice grammatical properties of the language.

• differentiation of tasks according to learners' needs

This is something that everyone would agree is a good idea in theory, but is often seen as impractical by hard-pressed teachers. For this reason, it is a practice seen more often in partnerships between mainstream and support teachers, and less commonly in one-teacher, large-class settings.

• encouragement of independent learning

This accords with the principle that education's broadest purpose is to enable learners to learn independently of the teacher, so that receptive skills tasks, for instance, need to engage the learners in heuristic processes: finding things out for themselves.

Oracy and Literacy

• noticing aspects of language form

Rather than relying only on English teachers to facilitate learning about how language works, the uses of language across the curriculum can offer material to do the same thing. All teachers can develop understanding about how language works within certain types of discourse, particularly those relevant to their own subjects, and they can construct their lessons so that their pupils can notice and practise the common features.

Receptive skills

• exposure to sophisticated, non-simplified subject material

Pupils are preparing for contexts in adult life where language is not simplified. In order to be independent in their ability to make sense of that language, and use it appropriately themselves, they have to be exposed to it. It is the tasks that they carry out as they are listening, reading, speaking and writing that can help them to manage the language, not a simplification of the discourse they are exposed to.

• variety of source material

In order to achieve this exposure, it is wise to use a variety of materials: written materials from real-world sources, eg. newspapers, and educational coursebooks; discourse spoken by the teacher, by visiting speakers, on video etc.

• the need for learner-training

It is possible to meet this through the use of 'ideational frameworks' and other devices, eg. visual representations of information, with which the pupils have to interact by labelling, ordering etc.

Productive skills

- the need for all pupils to take possession of the language of the subject

One cannot assume that learners will pick up the language of the subject by osmosis. They will need practice in it.

- closely guided and monitored groupwork

Groupwork facilitates many language development processes in ways that teacher-centred learning cannot. But groupwork must involve appropriate tasks leading to valid outcomes for it to be worthwhile.

- guidance in the processes of speaking and writing is possible, desirable and useful across the curriculum

- the need for practice in producing extended discourse

These are responsibilities which we might assume mainstream teachers of subjects other than English and Modern Languages would be nervous to assume. Nevertheless, in line with points above, they are ones that can be taken on.

The INSET courses were often the first time that the teachers had had an opportunity to focus on these issues, and on the 'ideational' way in which language carries information in subject areas. This was why we felt it was important to try to measure the impact of what we had done.

The impact study

We conducted thirteen interviews with staff from seven of the nine participating schools, and staff from the language support service. In each case the interview was structured and dealt with whole school/policy issues, departmental policy and practice, and individual teacher's feelings and practice. Six of the interviews were with individuals, and seven were conducted in pairs or groups of three and sometimes four. In all there were twenty six interviewees. We interviewed senior managers who had been responsible for deciding who should attend the training courses since we wanted to explore managers' impressions of any effects the courses might have had on practice in their schools. Similarly, we wished to interview the language support teachers and the head of their service to explore their perceptions of any changes that might be linked to the courses.

The findings

(As we quote, we introduce the teacher cited as 'she' irrespective of their actual gender, for the sake of anonymity.)

We counted comments concerning the pedagogic principles and related matters. We graded the comments as follows:

A   showing support for the principle, and evidence of application
B   showing support for the principle
C   showing awareness of the principle, but not positive support for it
D   lacking support for the principle
E   denying support for the principle

In general terms, one of the most encouraging findings was that the mainstream teachers in particular felt they had gained a great deal from the INSET courses. Just under 80% of their comments expressed support for the pedagogic principles, and over 67% of these included evidence from the teachers' own experience or materials.

Many of the interviewees recognised that putting the principles into practice effectively, particularly when they were relatively new, was time-consuming. Many of their reservations were related to issues like lack of preparation time.[3] But some of the mainstream teachers saw the techniques as time-saving in the long run, in that they got learners learning effectively, taking possession of the subject and the language that expresses it. A Science teacher, for instance, said this about an experiment-based lesson:

> When we got to the stage where they were just telling you what to do – you know they were using the correct names for the equipment and things – cos we'd spent that time on the language and sequencing.

By far the most significant of the principles proved to be those under the headings:

- Language across the curriculum
- Integrated pedagogic model
- Receptive skills
- Productive skills

Language across the curriculum

Sixty two comments were made relating to LAC. The majority of these (63%) were expressions of support for the idea, particularly at teachers' own individual level. For instance, a mainstream teacher said

> I think it's easy to think of yourself as a subject teacher but I think when you do focus on the language like that you can see that the concepts are more accessible to the children – so I think ideally I would like to see myself as a teacher of language.

On the other hand, out of seventeen comments made about the development of whole-school policies, eleven were to the effect that schools were not establishing LAC policies across the board, and that where language issues were being taken into account alongside subject content, it was usually much more strongly visible in certain departments (usually the English department) than in others. A teacher told us

> Within *this* school it's seen very much as part of the English department – I mean this is very much an English department initiative.

Integrated pedagogic model – significance of tasks

67% of the comments about the principles of *linkage* and the *usefulness of 'ideational frameworks'* showed enthusiasm for them. These are best exemplified by comments from three mainstream teachers – one of Science, and two of English.

> Using the grids and things – you know it's so appropriate to doing experiments and things that you can use it just on a day-to-day basis really.

> We do use grids and so on and tables as springboards for their oral work too – because they might brainstorm and actually fill in as a group – and again because they've got a framework there it's easier and they all chip in – because it is simply a grid you know – they're not put off by the fact that anybody's got to sit down – if they've got to record it's a tick they're recording.

> I used it with a book I used with Year 8 – and I used a flow diagram. We read a chapter – put a flow diagram on the board and immediately they were able to access the information.

Receptive skills

Of the comments about *the need for learner-training* in receptive skills 86% demonstrated that teachers strongly perceived this need, and the majority felt they could address it after attending the INSET course. A Science teacher explained a technique she had used:

> I've done a thing with the video where they've had a list and what they've had to do is put the number in order as it's appeared.

Addressing this need to focus receptive work often implies reviewing resources including worksheets. For instance, a teacher of IT and Geography said

> I enjoyed looking again at resources and seeing how better to structure them and make them more accessible to my pupils.

Productive skills

Over 81% of the comments about the importance of guidance and group-work were positive. Speaking about a lot of the pupils she teaches these days, a Science teacher claimed that

> They can't transfer what they're saying into written work but these sheets that we've used have actually helped them to do that.

The same teacher also recognised the value of collaborative groupwork:

> They're actually speaking when they're working out the answers in their pairs.

Other principles

Where other principles were addressed, it was usually because of the particular enthusiasm of the interviewee. For instance, the encouragement of *independent learning* through the use of the integrated pedagogic model was supported very powerfully by a mainstream English teacher:

> It gives them a much greater sense of achievement if they've unlocked something in that poem for themselves than if they've just had it explained to them – their self-esteem shoots through the roof.

The ideas that *spoken* and *written language* are each a *good medium for noticing and practising aspects of language form* did not excite much support. This is perhaps not very surprising, for two reasons. One is that mainstream teachers tend to see literacy, for instance, as the ability to associate the spoken word with the written word. The other is that subject teachers' attention is clearly much more on the value of language to communicate their subject than on the systems within the language itself. Of only seven comments on these principles, however, five were supportive. In fact, with reference to spoken forms, one of the Science teachers volunteered that she drills difficult technical terms:

> Quite a few of the children have problems saying the words so I get them to repeat it back to me now which I would never have done before – I'd have thought that would have embarrassed them – but now I get that child to say it and then I say 'Everybody say it now' – which is something I picked up on the course.

The advantages of *variety of source material* were noticed in all of the five comments made on this theme. A History teacher gave the example of how she had used a video about the First World War, and had designed tasks to focus the pupils' listening.

The principle of *productive skills practice for all pupils to take possession of the language of the subject* was accepted in five out of six comments made on this topic. A mainstream English teacher reported the following:

> I did something with finding quotes – it was a quote-quest where they had to fill in grids and things and they were using the Shakespearean language without even realising it – people were saying 'Have you found Thou art a villain?' – and I could hear it all the way around the room and it was brilliant.

(The Science teacher first quoted also espoused this principle.)

Fewer comments than we would have hoped were made about pupils' *need for practice in producing extended discourse*. On the other hand, four of the six comments made were supportive of the principle. A Science teacher extolled the virtues of the relationship between the use of 'ideational frameworks' (which she refers to below as *spending that initial time*) and the pupils' ability to produce appropriate extended writing. She was comparing the conventional approach adopted by Science teachers with the one she had developed from attending the course and learning from working with a language support teacher:

> If you think how long it takes [conventionally] for them to do the experiment with them keep asking you – then they've got to write it up and they keep asking you – whereas if you spend that initial time they just get on with it.

The idea of *exposure to sophisticated non-simplified subject material* received less support than we would have liked; just over half of the comments (four out of seven) demonstrated an inclination to simplify material that the children were to read or listen to, rather than simplifying the tasks that give them access to it. For instance, a History teacher said

> With a very low ability group my use of language changes totally – everything's a lot slower and much more basic.

Again, a Science teacher said

> I for one have become less reliant on textbooks that we buy in assuming that children can read them – and I tend to use them now only the barest minimum amount of time.

Finally an idea that met with hardly any support from anyone interviewed was that of the *differentiation of tasks according to learners' needs*; this was certainly because it was seen to require a great deal of preparation time.

Conclusion

All in all, the courses seem to have been seen as a success: the teachers and senior managers made many comments on their effectiveness. For instance, a Science teacher commented:

> I really enjoyed the course and I feel that personally – even if the school hasn't got a lot out of it – I did.

One principle that we have not mentioned as one of the main pedagogic principles, but which had clearly made an impression on various interviewees, was that of the use of bilingual pupils' home languages within the education context. 75% of comments on this were favourable, though most of this approval was for teachers' use of the home language to establish and maintain contact with the pupils, rather than use by the pupils themselves.

There was also a willingness to disseminate the ideas within and across departments, often using training materials based on those we had used during the courses. This was to be seen against a consciousness of the need for further staff development: for example, one mainstream teacher who had run an INSET day with members of her own faculty recounted the following experience.

> We developed on that day some working materials – staff went away and trialled those – then we came back together and discussed whether they'd been a success or not and revised ideas because we found that quite a few members of staff – although they might have tried those ideas – I don't think – because they'd not been on the [original] course – it's not as much in their mind if you know what I mean.

The ultimate aim of any in-service training, as with any training or education, must be to empower the recipients of that training. In some small way, perhaps this programme of courses has done so. Certainly, we would hope that the ultimate recipients – the pupils – will have benefited in various ways.

References

Bourne, J. (1997) The Continuing Revolution: Teaching as Learning in the Mainstream Multilingual Classroom. In Leung, C. and Cable, C. (Eds) *English as an Additional Language.* Watford: National Association for Language Development in the Curriculum (NALDIC). pp.77-88.

Bourne, J. and McPake, J. (1991) *Partnership Teaching: Co-operative Teaching Strategies for English Language Support in Multicultural Classrooms.* London: NFER/DES for HMSO.

Burgess, J. (1994) Ideational frameworks in integrated language learning. *System* 22/3: 309-318.

Burgess, J. (1995) 'Language support across the curriculum': paper presented at International Standing Conference for the History of Education, 17th Annual Conference, Berlin, September. Mimeograph CELSE, School of Education, University of Manchester.

Burgess, J. and Carter, I.G. (1996) Common codes for mainstream ESL support across the curriculum. *System* 24/2: 211-222.

Lock, G. (1996) *Functional English Grammar: An introduction for second language teachers.* Cambridge: Cambridge University Press.

Notes

1. Carol Barnard is now a Lecturer at South Trafford College of Further Education.

2. For details of the development of two complementary movements which have attempted to deal with the issues involved: the Language across the Curriculum movement and bilingual language support initiatives, see Bourne (1997) and Burgess (1995).

3. A senior manager commented that the mainstream teachers who were most likely to take on the responsibility of supporting their pupils' language development are those who are already 'confident' and 'comfortable' in the teaching of their subject.

PART 4: Developing tests together

CHAPTER THIRTEEN

Interculturality and English language paired oral exams: communication norms and their assessment

Jane Andrews and Richard Fay
University of Manchester

Introduction – A Collaborative Endeavour

This research involves three types of collaboration:

- on an intrapersonal level, collaboration between three professional hats we wear

- on an interpersonal level, interdisciplinary collaboration as colleagues

- on a broader level, collaboration with other parties involved in language assessment.

First, three interconnecting professional roles have sparked off this research project – we are both:

language teachers with experience of preparing students for exams such as the Cambridge First Certificate in English (FCE) and its paired oral Speaking Test (see Texts 1 and 2);

language assessors (eg. for the FCE) with an interest in 'communicative' exams (Text 3) and

teacher educators in language assessment and intercultural communication (Text 4) and our specialisms aid our reflections on language and assessment.

Text 1. First Certificate in English

- part of the Cambridge[1] Main Suite

- candidates are 'assumed to be able to do office work or take a course of study in the medium of the language being learned'

- divided into five papers

- Paper 5 Speaking Test (paired oral)

Text 2. Paired Oral (Paper 5)

- two candidates + two examiners (one interlocutor, one assessor)

- candidates may or may not know each other

- rating scales applied by both assessor and interlocutor

- Part 1 – short exchanges between each candidate and the interlocutor

- Part 2 – long turn from each candidate with brief reply from the other one

- Part 3 – candidates talk together

- Part 4 – candidates talk with each other and interlocutor

Text 3 'Communicative' Assessment

Speaking exams use linguistic criteria (eg 'pronunciation', 'grammatical accuracy' and 'range of vocabulary'). In recent years, communicative criteria such as 'interaction' and 'flexibility' have been added.

Text 4 Intercultural Communication

...acts of communication by individuals identified with groups who exhibit intergroup variation in their shared but individually expressed social and cultural patterns. (Damen, 1987: 37)

Text 5 Shared Concerns and Varied Perspectives

Common concern: silence in interaction.

Assessment focus: on hesitation whilst candidates search for ideas or language.

Intercultural communication focus: crosscultural variation in what is acceptable – what seems like an awkward hesitation to some may seem normal to others.

Second, we collaborate as colleagues teaching separate Masters-level modules to experienced English language teachers. The intercultural communication module reconsiders common assumptions about communicative language teaching in the light of recent intercultural thinking about communication. During this module, students acquire a questioning stance which they take to the language assessment module. This stance contrasts with the language assessors' desire for precision in the interests of reliability, validity, and practicality. Our students must therefore grapple with the differing approaches to 'communication' and similarly we seek common ground between our interest areas.

The two fields refer to different literatures and use terms distinctively. This tends to mask the common ground they share (Text 5). However, when a common concern can be identified and the different approaches to it can be shared, new interdisciplinary perspectives become available. In our discussions, many questions arise:

- how is silence interpreted in speaking tests?
- what norms are assessment criteria based on?
- what is a 'fluent' performance?
- what is appropriate turn-taking?
- to what extent are speaking tests 'natural' speaking contexts?
- what is effective task management?

Such questions led us to explore how a language assessor's approach to the 'communicative' aspect of language tests can be enriched with intercultural communication insights. To do this, we have chosen a context where communication is central: the assessment of speaking skills. We have chosen the paired oral FCE exam format because it involves non-native-speakers interacting with non-native-speakers (NNS). This type of interaction is of increasing significance as English is used more and more as an international lingua franca. With this focus, we have considered the following 'communicative' speaking test task from both a language assessment and an intercultural communication perspective:

> Two candidates are tested together; they must maintain and direct the discussion on their own (ie assessors do not participate); they have a collaborative task to complete which focuses on the process of communication rather than the outcome of the discussion (eg candidates need to choose a suitable educational course for someone with specified interests). The discussion, rather than the final decision, is the important feature. Candidates are told that assessment will be based on the way they express and justify their opinions and not just on the content of what they say.

For language assessors, positive features include the following:

- Candidates are placed in the relatively relaxed situation of interacting with a peer (as opposed to being faced with the unequal power relationship of interacting with the assessor) and thus will produce a range of language forms rather than merely responding to the assessor's questions

- The assessor is released from playing multiple roles during the exam (ie participant, assessor, manager of interaction) and can focus on assessment – this is important for reliability.

An intercultural communication perspective raises different issues:

- The task assumes that the interlocutor and assessor are non-participatory but their very presence is communicative, since the candidates' performances are affected by whatever meanings they attribute to these silent but present assessors

- The task depends on group formation and related communication norms but the stability of group norms depends on whether the groups are pre-formed or ad hoc formations

- The task requires the candidates to discuss the topic and come to a decision or consensus but the process by which this is achieved is dependent on the rhetorical norms of the candidates

- How is the performance of individual candidates within the group assessed? (According to agreed group-preferences, individual candidate preferences or implicit exam-defined preferences?)

The third type of collaboration resulted from our desire to see whether our hunches about the interaction in the paired oral are shared by experienced assessors and recent candidates.

Text 6. Research Stages

1) discussion of concerns shared by intercultural communication and language assessment

2) focus on the differing perspectives that intercultural communication and language assessment have of 'communication'

3) specific focus on the assessment of communicative performance in the FCE oral

4) baseline data gathering from experienced assessors and recent candidates

5) development of an intercultural communication conceptualisation of the FCE

6) focus on how experienced assessors operationalise FCE oral rating criteria

   (reported in this paper)

---

7) selection of Think Aloud as a research method; decision to work in standardisation settings rather than real exams

8) trialling three variations of the Think Aloud method with four assessors

9) running a pilot project using the preferred variation of the Think Aloud method.

This research arose from our professional practice and has developed into a project with a natural momentum (Text 6). The research focuses on the practice of paired oral assessors, their assessment criteria and their procedures. To find out more about this, we conducted semi-structured interviews with four assessors. We also interviewed paired oral candidates.

From these discussions three linked areas of interest have emerged. First, how do assessors and candidates regard the innovative paired oral exam format? Second, given that English is an international lingua franca (and that the paired oral format, with two NNSs interacting, emphasises this function), what are appropriate communication norms for paired oral performances? Third, what assessment criteria do assessors use to decide whether a candidate's interaction is effective or not?

Assessors' Perspectives

The assessors' comments open up a wider range of concerns than our hunches and take us beyond our narrow focus on the FCE oral. However, the following examples illustrate the emerging themes. Assessors generally like the paired format: Assessor 2 (A2) feels that the format has more benefits than drawbacks and is 'hugely worth it'. She compares the traditional 'one assessor-one candidate' format to a 'searchlight interview'. She remembers how long it would take to set the candidate at ease because the candidates were in 'interrogation position'. She also notes that candidates in this position are in 'rabbit mode', an image linking a rabbit blinded by car headlights to the candidate intimidated by the interrogation/interview situation.

The paired format does cause problems, however. For example, many candidates address the assessors rather than each other during the tasks, a natural enough tendency given the seat of power in the exam. A3 reveals her strategy for dealing with this: 'and sometimes I give little signals and I sort of go like this' [makes gesture to indicate 'talk together']. Assessors have some worries about the paired format such as the variable of personality differences: what happens when a 'bouncy' candidate is paired with a more 'solemn' one? Or when one candidate dominates? The candidates are also aware of this problem. Mismatching may also occur in understanding the exam context: one assessor (A3) feels that the paired format implies informality whereas it is really a formal exam. Her view is that assessors know, and so should candidates, that 'it's not a conversation and a chat'. This contrasts with the views of candidates who like the informality of the new format.

Thus, although the exam may appear as one thing (ie an informal chat), it has a different reality (ie a performance to be assessed). This can be understood in terms of the transactional purpose of assessors (ie 'give me some spoken language to assess') and the interactional perceptions of the candidates who have to relate to the strange (ie exam-dictated) communication of their assessors.

Assessors frequently use the metaphor of the examination as a game. Given the differences between the more traditional oral exam format and the paired format, the assessors stress the importance of candidates being well-prepared for what is expected of them. The game-related comments reflect a concern that candidates know the 'rules' of the game in question (ie the exam): 'whether students actually jump through the hoops that are set for them depends on their recognising those hoops'. At the same time, A2 feels that candidates are generally able to recognise what is expected in this particular game:

> The examining board – which has its own flavour its own social class its own social rules and it coincides on the whole with teachers' own sort of well-meaning middle class nicely educated middle aged largely southern – I could go on for ever you know! – we are a cultural sub group that's very recognisable and our students are not daft, they can recognise it.

Assessors can give examples of the kinds of 'rules' in use in the exam. After some consideration, A1 describes the rules she applies regarding the use of silence by candidates: 'you know, a ten second pause is enough from a European context, I'm thinking – anything longer is embarrassing'. A3 reflects on what she looks for in a 'good candidate' : 'I suppose I look at how at ease they are with the communication – I look at how much pain it causes me I think, so partly, it's my norms'. Only A2 noted candidates who appear to recognise what is expected in this game but do not play along with it. She comments on her personal response to this and her strategy for dealing with it during the exam:

> 'What they [the examination board] are presenting is a general purpose norm and I do understand why because it's the language of power – this is

useful language for people – I'm really torn about this you know I very often have candidates who don't play that game and I move myself into a different gear'.

Candidates' Perspectives

Since candidates have less experience of reflecting (in English) on their exam-taking experiences, we used a structured interview format to find out what they feel about the paired oral exam. As with the interviews with assessors, interesting themes emerged such as the awareness of how pairs of candidates (whether they knew each other or not) should operate, and the desirability of teachers preparing their students well so that they knew what to expect.

Regarding the candidates' attitudes towards the pairing, C5 is aware of the needs of her partner as well as her own in the exam:

> ...and it's important as well if you let – I was with a boy – if you let him speak – because sometimes you start speaking, speaking, speaking – and you didn't let your partner speak. Yeah, to work in a group – you are making – you are couples – you are making a couple – you are a pair – it's not only you or the other person.

Interestingly, C5 was paired with a candidate she first met at the exam but she felt very positive about the experience as the atmosphere between the candidates was not competitive. This contrasted with her previous experiences of paired orals. C2 shows a similar awareness of how the paired interaction should proceed: 'well I don't think it's good if you interrupt your partner – you listen to what he says – he/she says and say 'yeah that's right' – you have to talk with them'. However, C2 differs in her attitude towards the pairing. She was paired with a candidate she knew beforehand and preferred this: 'my partner was my best friend – so I was used to her dialect and so on'. C1 was paired with a candidate she already knew but felt that being with an unknown candidate would be unpredictable: 'I think it depends on the person – like – if you are having a partner that is a quiet person you can't help more – you tend to speak very much but if you are having a partner that is very talkative you can have lots to say about things'.

Text 7. Changing Norm-Generators

- native-speaker model (productive) candidates should sound like a native -speaker

- native-speaker model (receptive) candidates should be easily understood by native-speakers

- universal model which assumes that culture-neutral language use exists

- task-based model which assumes that a particular task (eg an interview) has generalisable expectations about linguistic behaviour

- emergent culture/facework model

Text 8. English as a Language of Wider Communication (ELWC)

Historical reasons (eg colonialism and emigration) and current pressures (eg technology-driven globalisation and linguistic-cultural imperialism) lead us to question whether the native-speaker orientation associated with the EFL model of English language use is still relevant.

However, when English is used as a Language of Wider Communication, what replaces the native-speaker norms?

Text 9. Culture-Free Norms

'this examination is set in the belief that there is a need to train learners to communicate effectively in language which is completely neutral, unmarked in any form by creed, race, culture, social status and the like ... This is, ... given the important role of English as a lingua franca in the world at large, the language of successful international communication.' (1990 JMB University Entrance Test in ESOL)

The candidates describe the exam as a positive experience compared to oral exams in their own countries. Much of their satisfaction stems from the preparation they received from their teachers beforehand. In C1's words: 'I think it – I'm OK because the teachers had already give me some clue about the oral exam so I didn't get nervous'. Candidates also gave credit to the atmosphere in the exam room. They comment on the fact that they are not conscious of the assessors writing notes about their performances. They also enjoy the tone of the exam as set by the interlocutor: what C1 calls friendly talk!'.

Assessment Norms

Over the years, language tests have embodied, explicitly or implicitly, differing assumptions about the model of communication against which candidates' performance is being assessed (Text 7). Native-speaker norms may still play a part today: 'candidates should be able to make themselves understood by the average native-speaker' as FCE examiners often express it. This assumes that native-speaker norms can be adequately identified (thus failing to recognise the intracultural diversity within 'native-speaker-dom'). They are also arguably inappropriate for exams like the FCE with their international orientation (Text 8). Finally, it denies learners the right to be themselves and instead forces them to 'plagiarise' the native-speaker culture (Kramsch, 1998). An alternative is to base norms on 'culture-free' communication (Text 9).

This assumes that we can identify language which is primarily transactional in nature. This is problematic for interculturalists who see communication in terms of meaning attribution:

> Communication may be defined as that which happens whenever someone responds to the behaviour or the residue of the behaviour of another person. When someone perceives our behaviour or its residue and attributes meaning to it, communication has taken place regardless of whether our behaviour was conscious or unconscious, intentional or unintentional. (Samovar and Porter, 1994: 7-8)

It also assumes that universal speech functions can be identified, a view challenged by work in crosscultural pragmatics (eg. Blum-Kulka et al eds, 1989) and critiques of anglocentric speech act theory (eg. Wierzbicka, 1985). Perhaps the universalism most commonly appealed to is that based on Grice's maxims (1975) such as 'avoid ambiguity'. However, such maxims are also coming under intercultural scrutiny (eg. Clyne, 1994: 194). Thus, for a value like ambiguity (and its avoidance) to be universal, universal agreement would be required about how explicitly meanings should be articulated, a requirement at odds with the basic ambiguous nature of communication (eg. Scollon and Scollon, 1995).

Another possibility is to derive norms from the tasks used to elicit the language required by assessors. Thus, the FCE paired oral begins with an interview-like first part in which the interlocutor asks the candidates a series of scripted questions about their backgrounds and preferences; can the norms be generated by the interview task type? Unfortunately, interview norms can also be seen to be culture-specific (eg. O'Grady and

---

Text 10. Interaction Descriptors

Typical communicative assessment criteria: the candidate:

- must be able to 'turn take' and 'direct' an interaction appropriately and keep it flowing

- shows only occasional lack of knowledge of 'conventional' ways of taking turns, but does not appear to be 'impolite'

- will take the 'initiative' when it is required.

Inverted commas = contentious areas.

Text 11. Holliday on Cultures (1998)

(1) 'Culture' ... is a concrete social phenomenon which is based essentially on the nation. Within the national culture, there is a complex of subcultures which vary according to the features of smaller groups, but maintain major national characteristics.

(2) 'Culture' is a movable concept used by different people at different times to suit purposes of identity, politics, and science. Thus, 'national cultures' are constructed by nationalism, 'ethnic cultures' by ethno-politics. In sociology, 'culture' is a methodological device to enable ethnography.

Millen, 1994) – is it more appropriate to 'sell yourself' or to demonstrate your 'humility'?

We are left seeking a source of appropriate norms, a situation compounded by the character of the more communication-oriented rating scales (Text 10). Although rating scales embodying communicative assessment criteria are to be welcomed, they have yet to grasp the cultural nettle with regard to norms-generation.

Intercultural Conceptualisation

This discussion of norms centres on 'culture' – not surprising if we adopt Hall's view (1959) that 'culture is communication and communication is culture'. Consequently, the cultural dimension to communicative language testing cannot be avoided. However, which understanding of 'culture' is most useful for us? Holliday (1998, 1999) argues persuasively for a disentanglement of two differing views (Text 11). Using Holliday, we can usefully distinguish 'large cultures' from 'small cultures'.

Large Cultures tend to be top-down, fairly fixed, national-level constructs which bundle all natives (eg. English native-speakers from Britain) into one mass. They thus oversimplify a complex picture with a culturalist, otherising stereotype. In language assessment terms, the link between a language and specified native-speaker norms is based on a Large Culture understanding. By contrast, small cultures tend to be emergent, fluid, small group constructs which are best understood through bottom-up description. Thus, to answer the question, 'What is the FCE paired oral exam culture like?', we need to observe and describe it before interpreting it. In language assessment terms, the current rating scale strategy of avoiding native-speaker norms seems to move towards a small culture understanding.

The second strand of our intercultural communication conceptualisation is built on the idea of communication as the attribution of meaning in which meanings are given by the observer to the behaviour of the performer. Thus when individuals interact (ie interpersonal communication), there is always an element of meaning negotiation. The need for meaning negotiation is magnified when the individuals concerned have differing backgrounds or expectations (ie intercultural communication). Intercultural communication and interpersonal communication are closely linked: interpersonal communication can be seen as the start of a cline which passes through intergroup communication, before reaching intercultural communication. Our interest rests on the communication of the paired oral candidates rather than on their backgrounds per se. We therefore emphasise the interpersonal dimension by thinking in terms of interpersonal communication across cultures (Gudykunst *et al* eds, 1996) rather than of simply intercultural communication.

Text 12. Face

[Face is] the conception of self that each person displays in particular interactions ... When a person interacts with another, he or she tacitly presents a conception of who he or she is in that encounter, and seeks confirmation for that conception. In other words, the individual offers an identity that he or she wants to assume and wants others to accept. (Cupach and Metts, 1994)

Text 13. Facework (Management)

Face is not merely what one individual dictates. Rather partners negotiate (usually tacitly) who each other 'is' with respect to one another. Each partner contributes to defining the identity that is expected to be displayed when they interact ... (Cupach and Metts, 1994: 96)

Text 14. Facework and Emergent Cultures

[Each partner contributes to] reaching a working consensus with regard to the face and behavioural line that each is expected to assume in particular encounters.

As a meaningful relationship develops, the working consensus evolves into a relational culture ... [that] is fluid and amorphous, but contextualises the meanings that each partner draws from his or her interactions. (Cupach and Metts, 1994: 96-97)

Successful meaning attribution involves negotiation of meaning and the negotiation of communication norms and roles; you are more likely to attribute meaning appropriately when you know who the other person is, how they want to be seen, how they view the interaction and the context in which it takes place. Equally, they need to know who you are, how you want to be seen, how you view the interaction and the context in which it takes place. This is a 'face' process (Text 12). The negotiation of mutually accepted and acceptable face is termed facework or facework management (Text 13). Facework is linked to the idea of emergent small cultures (Text 14).

The communication in communicative English language tests is, increasingly, lingua franca communication. We focus on that lingua franca communication – not on candidates' backgrounds or on a native-speaker cultural background linked to English. In the paired oral exam, an interactionist, emergent small culture is being created, and the exam is a facework site for interpersonal communication across cultures. We are arguing that the paired oral exams have their own cultural frame (the 'game'). This frame comes with hardware consisting of the exam design, tasks, materials, examiner and interlocutor roles. It also comes with a software consisting of the attitudes that candidates, assessors, exam writers, exam boards, teachers, and coursebook writers use as they attribute meaning to the exam hardware. Each exam performance takes place within this frame creating its own unique small culture whose characteristics emerge as the exam progresses. This emergent culture results from the facework management of the candidates, interlocutor and the silent assessor in the corner. It results too from their handling of the exam tasks.

We now have a new source of norms: the combination of the standard cultural frame used for all exams of the same type (eg. FCE) plus the unique emergent culture which is actually produced in a particular exam performance. We argue that assessors need to assess candidates' interactiveness in terms of communication norms appropriate to the exam performance they are involved in. This new understanding of the norm-giver may enable us to revise the way in which rating scales are understood and increase, through enhanced standardization procedures, the validity and reliability of the examiner-assessments without losing the important need for practicality.

Ongoing Research Directions

Our baseline research has encouraged us to continue working with experienced assessors and to find out more about their assessment practice. Insights into how norms are currently dealt with in 'English as a lingua franca' exams will raise issues as to how future and existing assessors can be trained and standardised in their work. This will contribute to our goal of seeing what intercultural communication thinking can offer to language testing.

Note

1   'Cambridge' refers to the University of Cambridge Local Examinations Syndicate (UCLES).

References

Blum-Kulka, S., House, J. and Kasper, G. (Eds, 1989) *Cross-Cultural Pragmatics: Requests and Apologies.* Norwood, NJ: Ablex.

Clyne, M. (1994) *Intercultural Communication at Work: Cultural Values in Discourse.* Cambridge: Cambridge University Press.

Cupach, W. and Metts, S. (1994) *Facework.* London: Sage.

Damen, L. (1987) *Culture Learning: The Fifth Dimension in the Language Classroom.* Reading, MA.: Addison Wesley.

Grice, P. (1975) Logic and Conversation. In Cole, P. and Morgan, J. (Eds) *Syntax and Semantics 3: Speech Acts.* New York: Academic Press.

Gudykunst, W., Ting-Toomey, S. and Nishida, T. (Eds, 1996) *Communication in Personal Relationships Across Cultures.* London: Sage.

Hall, E. T. (1959) *The Silent Language.* Garden City: Doubleday.

Holliday, A. (1998) Confronting Culture: Constraint or Resource? Plenary talk at the IATEFL Literature and Cultural Studies SIG Event, July 4th, Canterbury, UK.

Holliday, A. (1999) Small cultures. *Applied Linguistics* 20/2: 237-264.

Kramsch, C. (1998) The privilege of the intercultural speaker. In Byram, M. and Fleming, M. (Eds) *Language Learning in Intercultural Perspective: Approaches through Drama and Ethnography.* Cambridge: Cambridge University Press pp.16-31.

O'Grady, C. and Millen, M. (1994) *Finding Common Ground: Cross-Cultural Communication Strategies for Job Seekers.* Sydney: National Centre for English Language Teaching and Research, McQuarie University.

Samovar, L. and Porter, R. (Eds, 1994) *Intercultural Communication: A Reader.* (7th Edition) Belmont, CA: Wadsworth.

Scollon, R. and Scollon, S. (1995) *Intercultural Communication: A Discourse Approach.* Oxford: Blackwell.

Wierzbicka, A. (1985) Different cultures, different languages, different speech acts. *Journal of Pragmatics* 9: 145-178.

CHAPTER FOURTEEN

Reforming language examinations as classroom research:
washback and washforward in a cluster of teacher training colleges in Poland

Jane Andrews
University of Manchester

Jan Majer
Foreign Language Teacher Training College, Łódź

Donald Sargeant
British Council Regional Teacher Trainer

Richard West
University of Manchester

In this chapter we reflect on our experiences of collaborating on a language examination reform project in Poland from our perspectives as teacher educators and English language teachers based in the Polish and UK contexts. We report on the standardisation of assessment of the language skills of trainee teachers in the six colleges supervised by the University of Łódź in Poland. During the six-year life of a British Council-sponsored project, colleagues from the six Foreign Language Teacher Training Colleges (FLTTCs), represented by Jan Majer in this text, colleagues from CELSE, University of Manchester (Jane Andrews and Richard West), together with the regional teacher trainer (RTT), Donald Sargeant, revised the format and administration of the practical English exams. In the chapter, we draw parallels between the process of test development and of undertaking classroom research.

Introduction and Background

The prompts for the examination reform reported here can be traced to a variety of sources which need to be set out before the story of the examination reform project can be told. Firstly, a series of complaints were made by students at the FLTTCs about the final year examination format and content. Students who felt they were proficient in English were shocked to find that they failed their 'practical English' course and so they looked to their college lecturers to address a perceived injustice.

A second factor was the developing belief amongst the lecturers at the FLTTCs that their courses were distinct from those run by the local university department of English philology which had, up to that time, set the final examinations for the FLTTCs. This led to the conviction that the students' skills would need to be assessed in an innovative way and in a way which was more closely tailored to students' future language needs.

A third factor, related to the first, was that the examinations lacked standardisation and reliability. These should be essential characteristics of any high quality examination but were considered particularly necessary for an exam that would be taken by students across six different colleges and assessed by different college lecturers. Standards and criteria needed to be uniform.

The desire for reform was also prompted by an awareness amongst the college lecturers that, as future teachers, the students should experience good practice in both the content of their course and its assessment. In the context of the British Council-sponsored PRINCE project (see Chapter 11), the participants saw an additional benefit of the reforms as the professional development of the college lecturers involved in the process. An account of how the reforms were planned, put into place and monitored follows.

Collaborating on Examination Reform

The ethos in which the collaborative work was carried out under the PRINCE project has already been identified (in Chapter 11) as a key factor in its success. Collaboration played a crucial part in the examination reform work.

Collaboration was firstly at the institutional and international level: the colleges in the cluster, the British Council and the University of Manchester created a working relationship. The interaction between these groups with their 'insider' and 'outsider' perspectives on teacher education and assessment stimulated discussion and prompted the innovations outlined here.

Second was the collaboration among the colleges in the cluster, including the RTT who was based in the college at Łódź. This form of collaboration was novel in that although the colleges shared the common concern of training future language teachers, colleagues within them were unaccustomed to discussing their work and reaching agreement on a common approach.

Finally there was collaboration among individuals – when colleagues from the same college discuss issues, when colleagues from different colleges work together, when colleagues from the colleges work with the RTT, when Manchester colleagues work with college lecturers and when the RTT works with the Manchester colleagues. Collaboration between college lecturers was perhaps most noteworthy: in the early stages of the project, colleagues might have perceived their areas of academic specialism ('writing' or 'methodology', 'phonology' or 'literature') as distinctive enough to rule out any collaborative work.

Planning the new final year examination

At the first conference bringing together participants from all of the PRINCE link projects in Poland, held in Popowo in March 1996, many papers addressed the issue of assessment. West and Fletcher (1996) summarised the aspects of assessment which emerged as key and they are worth reproducing here in that they reflect the work carried out by the Łódź cluster.

Figure 1 indicates how test development needs to follow a similar process to a classroom research project. Planning, trialling, implementation, observation, reflection, analysis and future planning in the light of experience can be identified as essential stages in both processes. In the discussion that follows, parallels between a classroom research cycle and the test development procedure are drawn.

At the first cluster seminar (1994), some basic decisions were taken which represented the planning stage. The first was which of the four main examinations administered to students during their college career would be reformed first – the entrance examination, the end of year one and two examinations or the final proficiency examination? The idea of starting with the year one and two examination was rejected unanimously, as it was predicted that differences between students at the different colleges would be greater at the earlier stages of their studies, making agreement on standardised examinations difficult. The entrance examination was similarly rejected as it was developed by Łódź University and was beyond the control of the FLTTCs. These facts, and also the importance of the final year examination as a statement to external bodies of students' achievement and proficiency, encouraged the cluster to select this as their starting point for reform.

---

1. define objectives – skills/subskills/competences

2. identification of inspiring assessment models – task/text types

3. production of trial items/test papers/assessment procedures

4. selection of performance criteria and drafting of marking scales

5. trialling of assessment procedures and marking according to performance scales

6. redrafting and retrialling

7. selection of samples of students' performance matched to performance scales

8. assessor/trainer training and standardisation in use of assessment procedures and performance scales

9. publication and circulation of documentation – assessment procedures and performance scales (teachers and students)

10. evaluation

Figure 1: Summary of Issues in Polish Examination Reform in FLTTCs

Once this was decided, point 1 of Figure 1 was tackled and the cluster decided to change the whole format of the examination so as to meet the three challenges referred to at the beginning of this chapter:

- students would receive a grade which was a true reflection of their language skills

- lecturers would assess what had been taught and what they felt future teachers of English needed to be able to do

- reliability and standardisation could be improved.

We decided that the new examination would consist of five evenly weighted papers testing different skills and each accounting for 20% of the total grade. This would replace the traditional written and oral halves of the existing final year examination which each provided 50% of the total grade. The broadening of the examination was influenced by the desire to reflect the language skills identified as important for future teachers. In addition the new examination would be criterion-referenced as opposed to the existing norm-referenced procedure, which was arbitrary and unscientific. The differences between the new system and previous system are shown in Figure 2:

At the same cluster meeting, draft specifications for each of the papers were agreed upon. To ensure that all colleges would be stakeholders in the new examinations, and also to share the workload, teams from each college were asked to prepare sample papers from one or two specified areas and, where appropriate, marking scales. This work covers points 2, 3 and

'Old'		'New'	
Written	50%	Writing	20%
Oral	50%	Speaking	20%
		Listening	20%
		Reading	20%
		Use of English	20%

Figure 2: General Content and Weighting of the 'Old' and 'New' final year examinations

Paper	'Old' Content and Task Type	Paper	'New' Content and Task Type
Written	• 1 argumentative essay in response to a proposition (eg. 'Beauty is only skin deep') • lexicalised grammar test, multiple-choice, sentence-level format	Writing	2 part paper: part A involves 2 related tasks responding to input texts; one task is a formal letter, one task is an informal letter; B involves one piece of writing (an article or essay) in response to 1 of 5 tasks
Oral	• tasks varied according to examining board but could include 'read and respond to a text' or 'comment on a visual stimulus'	Speaking	• paired interactive format in sections following a warm-up • roleplay • problem-solving • discussion
		Listening	3 texts from authentic sources used to assess listening skills and strategies (eg listening for main idea, listening for gist)
		Reading	3 texts from authentic sources such as English language newspapers to assess reading skills and strategies (eg skimming, intensive reading, understanding gist)
		Use of English	tasks at sentence level and text level including proof-reading of authentic texts

Figure 3: Text and Task Types of the 'Old' and 'New' final year examinations

4 in Figure 1 and represented a substantial part of the cluster's work over a two-year period. This work was carried out during and between twice yearly meetings of all the project participants. Many innovations resulted from these meetings. Some examples of task and text types introduced into the newly-included skill areas are presented and contrasted with those used within the 'old' system in Figure 3.

Space does not permit an in-depth discussion of each innovation but one example is the radical reconceptualisation of the oral part of the examination. While under the previous system individual candidates would face a board of up to five participating examiners with unspecified roles (ie the student would address all examiners and any one could pose a question), it was decided that pairs of candidates would face a panel of three examiners, of whom one would interact with candidates while two remained in an assessment role. The aim was to replace the 'cross-examination' scenario with one in which candidates are encouraged to perform at their best. The implications of this new format for tasks and assessment criteria are discussed below.

College lecturers produced sample items according to the new final examination specifications. These were collated in Manchester in January 1995 ready to be discussed critically before the second cluster meeting in Łódź, in March 1995, attended by representatives from each college. At this stage we saw that it would have been much easier if all the papers had been produced at one college. However, the division of labour across the colleges was maintained so that the reforms would be more sustainable because of a wider sense of ownership, Secondly, there would be a cadre of trained testers in all the colleges by the end of the project.

At the March 1995 meeting, the project participants discussed point 5 in Figure 1: trialling items and assessment procedures. As in any research project, the trialling process emerged as vital in the production of a high quality, reliable and valid final year examination. Important issues emerged which had not been predicted, for example, the need to produce appropriate items for the 'use of English' paper. On the one hand, this appeared the least radical of the papers in terms of content and task types, on the other hand it presented the most difficulties in terms of the development of items at an appropriate level. Items which involved the translation of sentences from Polish into English were found to have low facility values, indicating that the level was too high for the students in the trial (a group of third year students from Łódź college). This task also proved to be extremely time-consuming to mark, due to the lengthy discussions necessary to achieve standardisation. Consequently the translation task was dropped.

The tests for the more subjective skills of writing and speaking were also trialled. For the writing examination the students' papers were marked by a panel of markers using criteria that had been agreed at the previous meeting. High levels of reliability were reached between markers, thus providing positive feedback on the tasks, criteria and expectations in terms of student performance. The trial indicated that word limits were too low for adequate performance on the tasks, so these were increased. Following this revision, model scripts illustrating performance at each point on the rating scale were selected and these were collated along with markers' comments, to produce a training manual for new markers.

Comments have already been made on the radical nature of the reforms of the speaking exam. During trials of the new format with willing volunteers from the third year student group in Łódź, oral performances were video-recorded and, with the permission of the students, marks using the criteria agreed by the lecturers were awarded. Assessors' marks were at the levels of 5, 4+, 4, 3+, 3 and 2, following the university requirements, on the criteria of fluency, accuracy, range, pronunciation, task achievement and interactive communication. Selected video performances were chosen by a panel of college lecturers as examples of performances at the specified levels in the same way that example scripts were chosen to illustrate the writing criteria. The scripts and videos were later used to train examiners in how to mark to the standard of the examination; as the examiners were college lecturers, it also indicated what was expected of students in this final year examination. Students were given access to the videos for the same reason.

Experiencing the new examination for the first time

The new examination was administered at the end of the 1994-1995 academic year. This represents the 'implementation' stage of a classroom research project. As with classroom research, observation and reflection led project participants to identify several areas requiring further attention. These areas are briefly outlined below with a more detailed discussion later in this section:

- the preparation of students in terms of familiarisation with the demands of the new examination (point 9 in Figure 1)

- standardisation of administration and marking procedures (point 8 in Figure 1)

- more extensive trialling of items and tasks (points 5 and 6 in Figure 1).

In the first case, some students felt penalised by not knowing what was expected of them in the new examination. In the second case, some markers appeared to have relied more on their intuition and previous experience when marking the writing paper than on the specified criteria, which led to great variation and a lack of standardisation of results across the cluster. Native English-speaking assessors were found to be more generous than their colleagues and the assessment of writing proved more time-consuming than predicted causing difficulties in meeting institutional deadlines for finalising grades. In the third case, it was found that certain items and tasks did not operate in the ways intended. Certain role-plays did not elicit a sufficient sample of language from both students; the answer keys produced for 'error detection' items on the use of English paper were unnecessarily rigid; on the listening paper when questions failed to mirror the order of appearance of the information in the text, confusion reigned and erratic results were noted.

Solutions to these three general areas of concern were devised by the cluster representatives and a summary is presented in Figure 4.

Between the first administration of the reformed examination in 1995 and the time of writing, three further examinations have been devised and administered and the cluster has worked together throughout this time with the RTT and Manchester on fine-tuning the examination. The next section reports some reflections from a range of participants on their experiences during the past five years.

Reflecting on experiences of examination reform

Throughout the process of reform, students (ie trainees) advised lecturers of their opinions of the innovations. This provided a useful balance to the perspective of the lecturers, who inevitably felt close to the innovation. From a classroom research perspective, the students' views acted as a form of triangulation, ensuring that differing viewpoints were accounted for in evaluating and reflecting on the new examination. Usually, students communicated their views either orally or via jointly-written letters to the lecturers working on the examination.

In 1997, attempts were made to capture in a more systematic way the responses to the reformed final examination of both students (through interviews) and lecturers (via paper-based and email questionnaires). The students involved in the interviews were second years who, by 1997, had experienced English examinations that had been reformed along similar lines to the final examination. Data gathering from college graduates was less feasible because people had dispersed after graduating. Data gathered from students and lecturers raised some interesting issues related to the experience of the new examinations and where improvements might be required.

The students' comments tended to reflect their fears about examinations but other issues coincided with points made by lecturers. The students' comments are summarised as follows:

- an initial sense of resistance was expressed to the reformed examination when students first encountered the changes

- students expressed doubts about the 'fairness' of taking examinations designed by 'external' lecturers (ie lecturers from other cluster colleges)

- doubts were expressed over how well the practical English courses 'prepared' students for the reformed examination

- students expressed their desire for a clear link between the syllabuses followed by each cluster college and the standardised examinations

- students wanted, above all, to be as well-informed as possible about the examinations in terms of requirements and criteria.

Problem		Solution
1	Students' lack of familiarity with format and content of new examination	• Students experience a 'mock' examination during their third year so that they know what to expect
2	Assessors' reliance on past experience and intuition rather than on specified criteria	• extra training of assessors is carried out
3	Overgenerosity of native English-speaking assessors on the assessment of writing	• native English-speaking assessors are paired with their Polish colleagues when assessing writing scripts
4	Difficulties in marking writing scripts within a short period of time	• the writing paper is rescheduled as the first of the examination period so that a longer period of time is available for assessment
5	Roleplays fail to elicit sufficient language from students	• roleplays are trialled more extensively
6	students' responses in use of English items contain correct answers not included in the answer key	• use of English items are trialled more extensively
7.	ordering of questions provokes underperformance by some students	• more attention is paid to the ordering of questions in listening (and reading) tasks and also more extensive trialling takes place

Figure 4: Solutions to problems encountered after the first administration of the new examination in 1995

Naturally enough, students' concerns were mainly with their own studies and grades. Nevertheless, there is some overlap with lecturers' reflections. The lecturers' comments were far more wide-reaching than those of students and, as the summary shows, some unexpected positive outcomes resulted from the reform work.

- the quality of the new final year examination was widely perceived as higher than the previous one

- how practical English was taught was modified as a direct result of the reforms

- mock examinations had been introduced to prepare students for the reformed examination

- students showed increased confidence due to better understanding of what to expect in the examinations, more positive attitudes towards examinations and greater respect for the examination as an accurate record of each student's command of English

- the process of reforming the examinations was noted as beneficial in allowing colleagues to co-operate within the cluster and to exchange ideas and experiences

Issues about communicating the requirements and format of the reformed examinations to students were noted by both groups and the new mock examination aimed to address this need. The willingness of the lecturers, who had the dual role of test developers and teachers, to consider how continuity could be ensured between courses and assessment procedures, is reflected in the comments above. Work on examination reform was seen to exert a positive influence on more than just the immediate area of assessment and the collaboration between colleagues was described by one respondent as a 'real asset'.

Looking to the Future

The achievements of the examination reform project in terms of process and product are evident. But how these initiatives can be sustained is problematical now that British Council funding has reached an end. In keeping with the creative ethos of the group, various ideas have been proposed, one of which is to establish an item bank to serve as a store of tried and tested tasks and test items for use in future examinations. Another suggestion is more email within the cluster to send and gather feedback on new items and ideas for tasks.

There are, however, concerns that without the catalytic function of project meetings with the participating groups individual colleges may return to producing their own in-house examinations. At the time of writing the cluster is in the early stages of preparing the first set of examinations outside the framework of the PRINCE project. Issues such as how continued collaboration can take place are being explored.

The current stage of the test development process in the FLTTCs is similar to the end of a cycle of classroom research, when one phase of an ongoing process has come to an end and a new phase is about to begin. As with a classroom research project, learning has taken place along the way about the process of test development and also the products, that is, the tests themselves. Finally, the collaborative nature of the project has encouraged the professional development of peers working alongside each other in a way which is noted elsewhere in this book.

Reference

West, R. and Fletcher, N. (1996) Summary of papers on examinations and assessment. In *Conference Papers of Popowo PRINCE Link Conference,* Warsaw: British Council.

CHAPTER FIFTEEN

From generic to specific: a genre-based approach to ESP testing

Richard West
University of Manchester

Anikó Tompos
Széchenyi István College, Györ, Hungary

Introduction and Background

English for Specific Purposes (ESP) has become a well-established branch of English language teaching in the past 25 years and a wide range of teaching materials has been designed in accordance with the learners' professional or academic needs. However, the institutional testing of ESP has raised a number of problems which have so far appeared insoluble. The fundamental problem is that of designing tests which assess the specific branches of English (English for law, English for medicine, English for agriculture, etc), while at the same time ensuring that the different tests are comparable in coverage and language level. How do we know that the test in, say, English for civil engineering is comparable with that in English for dentistry?

Three-way cooperation between a group of some fifteen institutions of further and higher education in Hungary, the British Council and the University of Manchester has led to innovations which suggest that there are solutions to the problems of testing ESP.

The Problems of ESP Testing

The starting point of ESP testing is validity: validity is the justification and starting point for most courses designed to teach English for Specific Purposes (ESP). Learners expect and even demand language input which is tailored to their professional or vocational needs: English for medicine,

English for lawyers, English for mechanical engineers, etc. In the words of Pilbeam (1987: 123): 'Is it valid? Materials written for and used by a particular target ESP group should mirror and reflect the ESP world of that group'.

Learners – usually adult learners – will reasonably expect their language examinations to reflect both the English they have been taught and the English they need for their studies or their professions, and these two should be the same. However, constructing valid examinations which satisfy the demand for subject-specific language courses raises two problems. The problem of practicality is simply the physical and intellectual effort needed to produce so many different examinations in the time available to hard-pressed language teachers. The problem of comparability involves seeking ways to ensure that all the subject-specific tests are actually assessing the same things at the same level. Put simply – are the different examinations of equal difficulty?

There have been various attempts to solve this problem. One approach has been to devise a single test which assesses the relevant language needs of a broad range of students but with content which is unfamiliar or neutral to all of them. This is the approach taken by the Northern Examinations and Assessment Board's University Entrance Test in English for Speakers of Other Languages (originally the Joint Matriculation Board's Test of English (Overseas)), which, for example, once asked students to produce a piece of writing on the evolution of eighteenth-century table legs from a series of pictures. It is argued that this approach is valid because all academic study involves handling new and unfamiliar topics. However, learners are unlikely to be satisfied that such topics are relevant to them, so regard them as lacking in validity.

A second approach is to devise a broad-spectrum ESP exam which covers the needs of a wide range of learners, usually by identifying a large test population and producing an exam which satisfies the common needs of all of them. This has been done with, for example, the University of Cambridge Local Examinations Syndicate's Business English Certificate (BEC), which tests business English at three levels and is widely used around the world. The disadvantage of this for learners is again to do with validity – the test does not assess the specific language skills that they have been taught and which they need in their future careers.

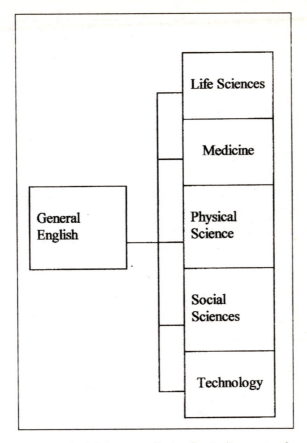

Figure 1: English Language Testing Service/International English Language Testing System

A third approach is to design modular tests, with separate versions for different specialist groups. The best-known example is perhaps the English Language Testing Service of the British Council, now known as the International English Language Testing System (IELTS). This originated in the late 1970s and students taking the exam could choose one of six specialist modules (see Figure 1). Although this approach has superficial appeal on grounds of choice and validity, in fact the specialist modules were unable to provide the degree of specificity that learners initially might have expected – doctors and medical students, nurses and paramedics all took the same 'Medicine' module. In 1995 the specific modules were abandoned and replaced by a 'general academic' module. Although the research shows that students have not been disadvantaged by this decision in terms of the scores achieved, there is an evident loss in validity with the loss of subject-specific modules.

The Service English Project (SEP)

It was against this background that the British Council's Service English project in Hungary established a testing initiative in 1998. The aim was to try to devise a test in English for Specific Purposes which would satisfy the demand for tests of specific English, yet without unacceptable burdens of impracticality and with assurances on comparability. The exam was needed by a number of university and other tertiary institutions which wanted to offer a foreign-language qualification as a graduation requirement. Typically, each institution specialises in a particular academic area – medicine, agriculture, law, engineering, and so on. Each institution then has a number of specialist departments and each department ideally wanted to offer a language examination tailored to its own needs. So, for example, a medical university would require separate exams in general practice, surgery, nursing, pharmacology, and so on. In all, some fifteen institutions have joined the project, covering a geographical spread across the whole of Hungary and an academic spread from agriculture to zoology.

The objectives of the project can be expressed in terms of validity, practicality and comparability:

- validity: to develop an examination system which will permit a language exam to be generated for any specialist academic or professional area

- practicality: to be able to generate a wide range of examinations without major investments of time or funds

- comparability: to be able to demonstrate that different versions of the examination are testing the same language skills at the same level, with high levels of reliability.

These objectives have, we believe, been achieved by adopting a new and coherent approach to the design, specifications, content and marking of the examination, now described.

Design and Specifications

C2 Mastery
C1 Operational Proficiency
B2 Vantage
B1 Threshold
A2 Waystage
A1 Breakthrough

Figure 2: Proficiency levels of the Council of Europe with SEP examination levels

It was first decided that the examination would be available at three levels and that these levels would have common definitions for all institutions and all specialisms. Because of Hungary's current political position of 'converging' with Europe ahead of accession to the European Union, three levels of the Council of Europe's *Common Framework* for language learning (1997) were adopted. These levels have been defined for general language proficiency, but the definitions needed adaptation to fit them to the academic and professional language requirements of ESP students.

Specifications were then developed which provide a blueprint for all examinations, ensuring that all components of all exams are designed, set, administered and marked in a uniform way. The examination has separate reading, writing, listening and speaking components, and specifications for the components cover:

- level of difficulty: which of the levels of the Council of Europe Framework is being tested

- purpose: the objectives of each paper

- timing: how long for each paper

- genres to be tested

- length of input (eg. reading or listening texts)

- source of input texts (usually authentic, professional or semi-professional)

- procedure: how each component of the exam is to be conducted

- rubrics: language of the instructions (always the target language)

- format: how many sections; which sub-skills are tested in each section; how many items in each section

- typical performance: what a passing candidate is expected to be able to do on each paper

- procedures and criteria for evaluation: training of markers, answer keys, mark allocations, criteria for marking writing and speaking papers.

Content

The paradox of developing a common examination with content which is specific for any academic, professional or vocational area now had to be faced. The solution to the paradox is what we call 'generic testing'. *Generic* in this context means two things: generic in the sense of including characteristics which are common to different areas, and generic in the sense of relating to genres.

'Generic' or 'template' items

Prototype items are produced and submitted to an editing committee. These items do not refer to any particular profession or academic area, but each item is generic in the sense that it can be adapted and detailed to provide 'specific' items for any such area. Each candidate is thus being tested on the same language skills in much the same way, but each item has been customised to suit his/her own particular specialism. For example:

Generic	Report (500 words) for professional(s) based on graph analysis and recommendation
1	Candidate is given a graph demonstrating a problem/trend
2	Candidate explains the graph and describes the trend
3	Candidate offers solution(s)/predictions

'Study the graph above. Write a report of 500 words for a colleague/superior/boss/meeting. Describe and analyse the situation, and offer possible solutions and/or evaluate future developments.'

Specific (Agriculture)

Statistics for small grain production in Hungary. You are preparing for a meeting of your agricultural company or institution. You are in charge of the small grains sector and you will have to report on your sector during the meeting.

Analyse the chart for small grain production figures for the last five years in Hungary. Based on your findings, write a report of 500 words describing the current situation and forecast possible future trends in the economy of your sector as regards the types of crops to be produced, land areas, marketability, also bearing in mind Hungary's accession to the EU.

Specific (Medicine)

Graph showing relationship between advantages/ disadvantages of drugs 1, 2, 3 in treating hypertension.

1   Candidate is given a graph representing the relationship between advantages and disadvantages of anti-hypersensitive drugs

2   Candidate explains and describes the graph

3   The candidate offers the best medication.

• Study the graph above and write a report of 500 words

• Describe and analyse the situation

• Offer recommendations on the best medication.

Specific (Business)

Graph showing level of disposable income in Far Eastern countries (downward trend).

Study the graph. Write a report of 500 words for a meeting of your company. Describe and analyse the situation and offer possible solutions to the problem it presents to your company in terms of export markets.

Specific **(Economics)**	Graph showing fall in share prices worldwide over the last year.
	Study the graph. Write a report of 500 words for your superior in your company/ financial institution. Describe and analyse the situation and evaluate future developments in share prices over the next 12 months.

This example of a writing item shows that it is relatively easy to take a prototype generic item and convert it into a range of specific items for any academic or professional area which are broadly comparable in terms of content. These examples are from varied fields, but it would be possible to take a generic item and produce specific items for more closely-related disciplines such as medicine, nursing, paramedical services, pharmacology, etc. It can also be seen that the test experience of candidates taking different versions of the same exam is comparable in several ways: the input received by each student (instructions and a graph) is comparable, the language skills tested (writing a professional report) are comparable, the output is comparable in terms of genre and length (a report of 500 words), and also the marking criteria are comparable (overall writing, grammatical accuracy, lexical accuracy, appropriacy and register, coherence and organisation, and adequacy/relevance of content).

Testing of genres

The tests are also 'generic' in that items are based on widely-used genres in various professional fields. Genres were chosen rather than, say, grammatical items, functions or language skills because they represent what students will have to do with their English in the professional world after graduation. And genres are understood by all parties in the professional equation: specialist teachers, English-language teachers, students and working professionals, making it is easy to discuss the content and results of the tests.

Research by the second author established a list of agreed spoken and written text types or genres employed by all professional areas (see Figures 3 and 4). This list was drawn up after first reviewing the current research and literature and then consulting professional engineers to draw up an initial list of technical genres. Next this list was submitted to ESP teachers of all specialisms involved in the SEP project, discussed and refined. In

> **GENRES (LISTENING and SPEAKING)**
>
> - introduction to place of work, office, laboratory, production unit, machines, etc
>
> - introduction to own job, responsibilities, working conditions, etc
>
> - description and explanation of equipment, processes, etc
>
> - warnings, eg safety precautions
>
> - instructions, eg operating instructions
>
> - professional telephone conversations (professional-professional)
>
> - professional telephone conversations (professional-non-professional)
>
> - professional telephone conversations (non-professional-professional)
>
> - interviews (professional-professional)
>
> - socialising, personal conversations
>
> - consultations (professional-professional)
>
> - consultations (professional-non-professional)
>
> - negotiations (professional-professional)
>
> - negotiations (professional-non-professional)
>
> - professional meetings/workshop discussions
>
> - professional talks/presentations (to professionals)
>
> - professional talks/presentations (to non-professionals)
>
> - academic lectures (exhibitions/conferences)
>
> - hand-outs (at conferences, meetings, etc)
>
> - notes (taken at meetings, training sessions, etc)

Figure 3

GENRES (READING and WRITING)

- warning labels/safety instructions
- notices, memoranda, internal messages
- advertisements (eg job advertisements)
- operating instructions
- product/service descriptions, design specifications
- manuals (eg operating manuals)
- price lists and catalogues
- initiative letters (to professionals/non-professionals)
- responsive letters (to professionals/non-professionals)
- faxes (initiative/responsive)
- e-mails (initiative/responsive)
- forms and pro-formas
- applications, bids and tenders
- proposals, recommendations
- minutes of meetings
- reports and professional memoranda
- analytical reports (studies)
- contracts
- patents, certificates, statutes
- job profiles
- curriculum vitae/resumés
- articles and notices for company bulletins/in-house journals
- articles in semi-professional journals, trade journals, press releases
- articles and abstracts in professional and research journals
- reviews of professional books
- professional/scientific books
- professional/scientific textbooks
- reference materials (eg encyclopedia entries/articles)
- poster presentations (at exhibitions/conferences)
- hand-outs (at conferences, meetings, etc)
- notes (taken at meetings, training sessions, etc)

Figure 4

several cases different names were used for the same genre (a *professional consultation*, for example), or the same name used for different genres (for lawyers *reports* and *instructions* are very different from reports and instructions in other fields). Narrow conventions for structuring and displaying genres also differed somewhat. Nevertheless, genres gave us the common currency that the project needed. It has enabled project members to devise teaching syllabuses based on genres, and so ensure that the teaching from one institution to another or from one department to another is broadly comparable in terms of coverage. It has also enabled item writers to devise 'generic' items which always take a particular genre as the starting point: the genre of the item is always specified, together with a brief outline of the content, additional input information that is to be supplied to the candidates, and the treatment in the task. This 'generic' item is then converted into specific items, always based on the same genre.

Conclusions

The objectives of the project were to devise a generic examination which could be adapted to the much narrower requirements of particular institutions, departments and even courses. The use of generic items forms the basis of the claims for comparability between different versions of the exam used in different institutions; the use of specific items generated from those generic items ensures validity, as each student is using a version of the test which has been customised for his/her own professional or academic area. The generation of specific items from generic ones is relatively quick and easy, ensuring that the exam is practical for teachers to devise.

The project is currently in the pilot stage, with all institutions cooperating in the drafting of items, the construction of trial papers, and the trialling of those papers. This trialling has not only allowed us to refine the papers and testing procedures and to devise a guide for item writers, it has also enabled each institution to gain experience in conducting the exam and observing how its students perform on this type of examination. A final interesting development has been the beginning of cooperation with other languages and it is hoped that the next round of trialling will include papers in German for specific purposes with support from the Göethe Institut.

References

Council of Europe (1997) *Modern Languages: Learning, Teaching, Assessment – A Common European Framework of Reference*. Strasbourg: Council of Europe.

Pilbeam, A. (1987) Can published materials be widely used for ESP courses? In Sheldon, L. (Ed.) *ELT Textbooks and Materials: Problems in Evaluation and Development*. ELT Documents 126: 119-24.

Index

207